"I found this book riveting,  ;iven so much of his life to really h... :o their questions and is deeply eng;... ns. The result is a book that profou... going on beneath the surface in ou...

Rico Tice, Cofounder, Christianity Explored; author, *Capturing God*; *Finding More*; and *The Ultimate Christmas Wishlist*

"Atheists like me, and other religious skeptics, are sometimes quick to dismiss popular apologies of traditional Christian faith. But this can be unfair, and in the case of Randy Newman's new book, it would be. The book is well argued, well informed, and thought-provoking. It is also, I might add, not Pollyannaish. Newman readily acknowledges the weaknesses and uncertainties of some of his arguments but insists that the other side faces even greater problems. As to whether he successfully makes his case—well, the issues here are complicated. Newman does make a strong case that the virtues of faith cannot easily be dismissed. But the virtue that I think matters most is epistemic virtue. Does faith produce knowledge, or at least rational belief, more rational than its denial? Newman offers some interesting and thought-provoking arguments that it does, but I don't think those arguments ultimately succeed. Still, the book is worthy of serious consideration, and I very much recommend it, including to religious skeptics like me."

Emmett L. Holman, Associate Professor Emeritus of Philosophy, George Mason University

"A book like this will be enormously helpful, and Randy Newman is the right person to write it. *Questioning Faith* addresses many of the questions people ask as they consider Christ, and it does so with insight, compassion, sensitivity, and humor. I expect I'll be giving away copies often."

Mike McKinley, Pastor, Sterling Park Baptist Church, Sterling, Virginia; author, *Friendship with God*

"Cynicism and unbelief are easy, particularly when they are trending. But then what *do* you believe? Do you have any roots or anchor, or do you drift with the ever-changing sentiments of society? Do you have any solid, satisfying hope, any spark of joy in your soul deep enough to withstand life's successive waves of disappointment and pain? Randy Newman is a reliable voice to engage people who are questioning faith and looking for lasting answers. He himself has journeyed through terrains of doubt. He knows how to help the fainthearted. He has mercy on those who raise tough questions. He has patience to follow the twists and turns of your own story—and to invite you to explore ultimate questions about its destination."

David Mathis, Senior Teacher and Executive Editor, desiringGod.org; Pastor, Cities Church, Saint Paul, Minnesota; author, *Rich Wounds*

"In a time of instant outrage, Randy Newman delves into the most divisive of topics with refreshingly earnest, patient, and contemplative attention. This book offers an examination of the self whose usefulness extends far beyond the scope of religious discourse alone. This exploration of faith and the human experience is a great model for how to learn about yourself and the world through discourse."

Samuel Nealy, Assistant State Director, Virginia, American Atheists

"I remember searching for inner peace. Even more, I was hoping to find some way of making sense of my life, the modern world, and my Jewish upbringing. Somehow, I knew in the depth of my soul that part of the solution to these deeper questions would involve my Creator. I was raised to believe in God, but in fact I was far from faith. It is too bad *Questioning Faith* was not around at that time, as it would have sped up the discovery of an intimate and personal relationship with God that I have enjoyed now for many years. If you are searching, Randy Newman's new volume will help you find what you are looking for—and more!"

Mitch Glaser, President, Chosen People Ministries

Questioning Faith

Other Gospel Coalition Titles

For Those Who Don't Identify as Christians

Confronting Christianity: 12 Hard Questions for the World's Largest Religion, by Rebecca McLaughlin

Confronting Jesus: 9 Encounters with the Hero of the Gospels, by Rebecca McLaughlin

Does God Care about Gender Identity?, by Samuel D. Ferguson

Is Christianity Good for the World?, by Sharon James

Remember Death: The Surprising Path to Living Hope, by Matthew McCullough

For Confessing Christians

Finding the Right Hills to Die On: The Case for Theological Triage, by Gavin Ortlund

Growing Together: Taking Mentoring beyond Small Talk and Prayer Requests, by Melissa B. Kruger

Keeping Your Children's Ministry on Mission: Practical Strategies for Discipling the Next Generation, by Jared Kennedy

Mission Affirmed: Recovering the Missionary Motivation of Paul, by Elliot Clark

The New City Catechism: 52 Questions and Answers for Our Hearts and Minds

Rediscover Church: Why the Body of Christ Is Essential, by Collin Hansen and Jonathan Leeman

Why Do We Feel Lonely at Church?, by Jeremy Linneman

You're Not Crazy: Gospel Sanity for Weary Churches, by Ray Ortlund and Sam Allberry

For Children

Arlo and the Great Big Cover-Up, by Betsy Childs Howard

Meg Is Not Alone, by Megan Hill

Polly and the Screen Time Overload, by Betsy Childs Howard

Lucy and the Saturday Surprise, by Melissa B. Kruger

To explore all TGC titles, visit TGC.org/books.

Questioning Faith

Indirect Journeys of Belief through Terrains of Doubt

Randy Newman

:: **CROSSWAY**®

WHEATON, ILLINOIS

Questioning Faith: Indirect Journeys of Belief through Terrains of Doubt

© 2024 by Randy Newman

Published by Crossway
   1300 Crescent Street
   Wheaton, Illinois 60187

Cover design: Faceout Studio, Amanda Hudson

Cover image: Shutterstock

First printing 2024

Printed in the United States of America

Trade paperback ISBN: 978-1-4335-8923-2
ePub ISBN: 978-1-4335-8926-3
PDF ISBN: 978-1-4335-8924-9

Library of Congress Cataloging-in-Publication Data

Names: Newman, Randy, 1956– author.
Title: Questioning faith : indirect journeys of belief through terrains of doubt / Randy Newman.
Description: Wheaton, Illinois : Crossway, 2024. | Series: The gospel coalition | Includes bibliographical references and indexes.
Identifiers: LCCN 2023013626 (print) | LCCN 2023013627 (ebook) | ISBN 9781433589232 (trade paperback) | ISBN 9781433589249 (pdf) | ISBN 9781433589263 (epub)
Subjects: LCSH: Faith. | Faith (Christianity) | Trust in God—Christianity. | Christian life.
Classification: LCC BV4637 .N485 2024 (print) | LCC BV4637 (ebook) | DDC 234/.23—dc23/eng/20230808
LC record available at https://lccn.loc.gov/2023013626
LC ebook record available at https://lccn.loc.gov/2023013627

In memory of Greg Boros,
dearly loved,
greatly missed

Contents

Introduction

Through Many Twists and Turns

YEARS AGO, MY SON DAVID AND I scaled the challenging Angels Landing Hike in Zion National Park. It's only a little over two miles from the parking lot to its magnificent zenith. But the climb conquers over sixteen hundred feet in elevation gain, earning it the distinction of "challenging" in every hiking guidebook you can find. (Truth in advertising: we did not attempt the final half mile, where hikers need to cling to chains to prevent falling to their death—as fourteen people have done since the year 2000!)

At one point, while gasping for air, I asked some climbers passing us on their descent, "How much farther?" They smiled politely and offered encouragements like "You can do it" and "It's well worth it." I doubted their reports. A bit later, we arrived at the intimidating start of twenty-one switchbacks known as Walter's Wiggles. Staring straight up at these zigzag paths of the final ascent of 250 feet, I really hoped it would be "well worth it."

Switchbacks are ingenious inventions to make steep mountain climbs possible. The *Merriam-Webster Dictionary* online defines a switchback as "a zigzag road, trail, or section of railroad tracks for climbing a steep hill." Had it not been for Walter's Wiggles, I would have needed six more hours, several oxygen tanks, numerous climbing ropes, or—forgetting all that—a helicopter! Though not easy, switchbacks make the task less difficult. Sometimes the indirect route, through many twists and turns, is the best.

When we arrived at our goal, Scout Lookout, we gazed down at the tiny parking lot where we began our hike. Were those people or ants down there? Then we began our descent—far less rigorous but no less glorious. In fact, the views we could now take in, no longer gasping for breath, made the entire experience one of the highlights of my life. Surprisingly, we noted several other series of switchbacks we had failed to recognize on our way up. These were more gradual than Walter's Wiggles, thus more subtle. Sometimes, when you look back over a past event, you see things you hadn't noticed before.

Indirect Journeys of Faith

This book is about spiritual journeys, not mountain climbing. But, after listening to hundreds of people's stories of faith, throughout more than forty years of serving as a kind of spiritual guide, I've come to see that spiritual journeys resemble a series of twists and turns more than a direct ascent from one belief to another. My own story certainly fits that description. (I'll share more about my wanderings later.)

Some of the stories I've heard move from unbelief to faith. Others move in a variety of other directions. Quite a few travel through terrains of doubt. I find them all fascinating and illuminating. I think they have a lot to say to a lot of people. They can point searchers in helpful directions. They can encourage weary travelers to keep going. Each chapter that follows shares several people's stories and tries to identify common themes that tie them together.

Maybe you've picked up this book because you once had faith but haven't for a while. Or perhaps you've never had faith and now wonder if it's worth considering. Or maybe you've been part of a faith tradition and find some of it unsatisfying. Then again, maybe you just love good stories. Some narratives might resonate with your own experience or reignite your search or remind you of what was good before you disconnected from spiritual pursuits. Stories of faith can challenge assumptions that stymie the process of searching for answers. Whatever your motivations, my hope is that the stories I recount in this book can help you as you step into the next chapters of your own story. But before someone's story can be helpful, we must be willing to listen.

Will You Listen?

My father fought in World War II, serving in the Coast Guard on a ship in the Mediterranean Sea. He actually served on three ships—German U-boats sank the first two. I remember hearing my father recount dozens of times when his first ship was torpedoed and sinking. He and his crewmates clung to life vests or flotsam or whatever they could find for thirty-six hours, waiting for rescue ships to arrive. Astonishingly, the horrors of that situation never hit me while my father told the story. *There goes Dad again*, I thought, *telling that story of floating in the Mediterranean.* I cringe now as I admit my callous heart.

What must it have been like to grasp desperately to a floating hunk of wood or something equally flimsy, wondering how long you could hang on before drowning? While my father and his crewmen waited those thirty-six hours, it wasn't as if they had booked a rescue squad. No one assured them: "Just hang on guys. We only have a few more hours before they get here!" They had no idea if anyone anywhere knew their ship had been sunk or that survivors were floating and waiting for rescue. Did some of them fail to hang on and drown? That seems almost certain. Did my father watch comrades slip into the sea, never to resurface? It's hard not to assume so. How many didn't survive? Most? How many persevered and climbed aboard a rescue ship—waterlogged, starving, and barely able to move?

It's possible to hear a story but not really hear it. In fact, repetition may not wake you to the reality of the story. The repeated telling might increase the dullness of hearing. Some of my deafness to my father's stories came from the culture of anti-war sentiment in which I was raised. Whether we realize it or not, what saturates the culture around us influences what we accept inside us. The same can happen with stories of faith. We can hear them so often, we grow deaf to them. Or our current climate may overshadow our desire to consider different perspectives.

Consider these confusing cultural factors that can keep us from listening well when someone shares his or her spiritual journey:

1. Many religious traditions are declining or merely maintaining their numbers today, but one category is skyrocketing— the "nones." Those who say they have no particular religious belief have grown in the US from 5 percent to at least 30

4

percent in the last forty years.[1] Are you in this category? If you were asked in an online survey about your religious beliefs, which label would you select from the multitude of choices in a drop-down menu?

2. The category labeled *evangelical,* a camp that once defined itself with specific Christian beliefs, now has people signing on from Jewish, Muslim, Roman Catholic, and agnostic perspectives. They define *evangelical* primarily as a political category.[2] What do the words *evangelical* or *Christian* mean anymore? Do they mean anything at all?

3. An atmosphere of doubt and cynicism pervades our society. You may have noticed that many people "get their news" through comedians who feel no need for accuracy or fairness, so long as their material gets laughs. We could debate whether the comedians are a forming influence on our society or merely reflect a culture that is already cynical, but there's no doubt that irony and skepticism shape many aspects of peoples' lives, including their spirituality. As journalist Adam Gopnik observed, "Modern people are drawn to faith while practicing doubt, as our ancestors confessed their doubts while practicing faith."[3] Does this generally skeptical attitude describe you?

Somewhat surprisingly, given the skepticism and confusion of our culture, a lot of people still pursue spiritual answers. Recent

---

1 Ryan Burge, "Why 'Evangelical' Is Becoming Another Word for 'Republican,' " *New York Times*, October 26, 2021, https://www.nytimes.com/.

2 Burge, "Why 'Evangelical.' "

3 Adam Gopnik, introduction to *The Good Book: Writers Reflect on Favorite Bible Passages*, ed. Andrew Blauner (New York: Simon and Schuster, 2015), x.

research found that a high percentage (79 percent) of people who do not affiliate with any religion are very willing to discuss the topic with a friend—if that friend takes his or her faith seriously.[4] My hope is that you're one of them, that you'll listen to the stories that follow with open ears and an open mind. Like my climb up Walter's Wiggles, it may just be "well worth it."

4   Rick Richardson, *You Found Me: New Research on How Unchurched Nones, Millennials, and Irreligious Are Surprisingly Open to Christian Faith* (Downers Grove, IL: InterVarsity Press, 2019), 58.

1

The Question of Motives

What If We Aren't Blank Slates?

CHRISTOPHER HITCHENS, the famed atheist, converted Alex.[1] In fact, he converted him twice. From the time he was just fourteen, Alex devoured Hitchens's scorching atheist rants in *Vanity Fair* and on an ever-expanding list of skeptical websites. Raised in a rural, anti-intellectual community, Alex grew in rage to match the wrath of his hero, the author of the bestselling *God Is Not Great.*

I knew none of this when I first met Alex. He was twenty-five at the time and worked for a Christian organization in the same office building where I worked. When I asked him how he got connected to a Christian organization, he told me about his two conversions. I was intrigued. He began with Hitchens. Two journeys—Alex's and Christopher's—shape this chapter

1   Not his real name.

and help us consider the question of motives. They show us that we all bring more to the table than mere intellectual curiosity.

Alex loved the ways Hitchens mixed brilliant articulation with piercing wit. Alex felt proud in rejecting his parents' Christian faith, his so-called Christian school, and, as he described them, other "knuckle-dragging Baptists" he knew. Watching hours of YouTube videos of Hitchens skewering his opponents armed him with both substance and style for ridiculing hypocritical Christians.

Hitchens wasn't just an atheist. He called himself an "antitheist" and bombarded religious people with relentless attacks, bolstering his claim that "religion poisons everything."[2] Older atheists like Bertrand Russell engaged in philosophical arguments that were out of reach for most nonacademics. They seemed tame compared with Hitchens and other so-called new atheists. Hitchens held back nothing. He even wrote a tirade against Mother Teresa. For Hitchens, nothing was beyond the pale. And Alex ate it all up with glee.

As Alex recounted his journey from presumed faith to rejected faith to newfound faith, I kept wondering if there was more to the story than mere changes in intellectual beliefs. In addition to rational arguments, I wondered what other dynamics contributed to this journey. I'd heard enough personal stories to know they include more than just logic and reason. We're whole persons, not just brains on a stick. And we approach the topic of faith with a menagerie of motives, not just intellectual curiosity.

2   Christopher Hitchens, *God Is Not Great: How Religion Poisons Everything* (New York: Twelve, 2007).

Below the surface, Hitchens's message resonated with Alex for more than just intellectual reasons. They both saw and experienced disgusting hypocrisy in the Christianity they were immersed in from childhood. For Hitchens, it came through a nominally Christian school in the UK. For Alex, it permeated a nominally Christian school in the southern US. Both settings failed to live up to the Christian mottos on their walls and the sermons preached in their chapels. Both schools' administrations merely winked at sexual abuse, leading both young men—Hitchens and Alex—to declare themselves atheists before the age of sixteen, with no shame or felt need to justify the newfound label.

"Hitchens gave me reasons to believe what I believed," Alex told me, quickening his speech. "More than that, he provided a replacement for the Christianity of my upbringing, an all-encompassing worldview without holes. Atheism also gave me approval to live the way I wanted." The connection dug deeper than just ideology. "Hitchens was full of rage and so was I," Alex continued. "It was as if he dismissed Christianity for the same reasons I had. Both of us rejected the so-called Christian faith we saw at our schools and said: 'If that's Christianity, I don't want it. And *no one* should want it.'"

At that point in our conversation, Alex paused and shook his head in what looked like unbelief. I asked him what was going on inside him and he struggled to find words. "I'm kinda amazed," he began. "So many twists and turns. I really was a very different person. I almost don't recognize that guy back there." I'd heard these expressions of contrasting personhoods before. Even so, I found Alex's story unique. Our journeys often manifest commonalities with others'. Yet, somehow, every story is unique. There is only one trail to the top of Angels Landing in Zion National Park. But everyone's experience up that path is distinct.

Christopher Hitchens's journey to anti-faith involves more ingredients than just intellectual disagreement and condemnation of hypocrisy. In his memoir *Hitch 22*, he gives ample space to sexual experimentation outside the bounds of traditional morality with no accompanying guilt. Finding those experiences pleasurable, he gained fuel to mock the intolerance of anyone who condemned *any* sexual expressions simply because of religious prejudices. Hitchens went further. "I always take it for granted that sexual moralizing by public figures is a sign of hypocrisy or worse, and most usually a desire to perform the very act that is most being condemned."[3]

The Story behind the Stories

One other trauma may have contributed to Hitchens's atheism, although the link may not seem immediately apparent. In his memoir, he detailed a fond affection for his mother while disdaining his cold, "morose" father. His painful recounting of the horrific suicide of his beloved mother may point to an iceberg of which his public debates against Christians was only the tip. In a radio interview upon the release of *Hitch 22*, Hitchens summed up that episode and its effect on him this way:

> My father was, as you say, a lifelong Navy man, so I had this rather morose Tory in my background who was hit off bril-

3   Christopher Hitchens, *Hitch 22: A Memoir* (New York: Twelve, 2010), 78.

liantly, by contrast, by my mother, who I always called Yvonne. And I call her Yvonne in my chapter, because it's a stylish name and because she was a stylish girl.

And her story's a tragic one and it ended tragically, in that having waited I think rather too long, because divorce and separation were extremely frowned upon in that set in those days. She did take up with another man after my brother and I had grown up, and it didn't quite work out. In fact, it didn't work out at all. And they made a decision to put an end to their lives and committed suicide together in Athens.

I think I had a chance to save her and failed to grasp it. She tried to call me from Athens and failed. Though I might have just missed the call by a few minutes, I don't know. But I've always been certain that if she'd heard my voice, she wouldn't have done it. So I've been trying to write my way out of that ever since.[4]

"Trying to write my way out of that ever since." Can you imagine the pain just below that surface? Hitchens was renowned for his capacity to consume alcohol. Is it possible that self-medication for emotional pain explains more than just a preference for the taste of Johnnie Walker Black?

Unexpected and Unwanted Turns

At some point, Alex's delight in Hitchens took a surprising detour. Hitchens condemned large numbers of people who didn't agree with his political views (like his support of the Iraq

4 Christopher Hitchens, in "Christopher Hitchens' Unusual and Radical Life," interview by Scott Simon, NPR, June 5, 2010, https://www.npr.org/.

War), always claiming a kind of moral high ground. But Alex wondered how he could do so. To word it the way Dostoyevsky did in *The Brothers Karamazov*, "If there is no immortality of the soul, then there is no virtue, and therefore everything is permitted." And "if there's no infinite God, then there's no virtue either"[5] and, by extension, no objective basis to condemn anything. Alex wondered what foundation Hitchens used for his moral pontifications. Suddenly his hero seemed a little full of himself.

Alex wasn't the only one who observed this inconsistency. More and more public figures poked at what might have been a chink in Hitchens's armor, asking, "If there is no god, on what basis do you make moral judgements about right and wrong?" Hitchens dismissively and repeatedly responded:

> Morality is innate in human beings. . . . Religion didn't create morality or make moral judgments first. People found morality within themselves and religion followed. . . . The awareness of the difference between right and wrong is innate in human beings . . . and it can be observed . . . in societies where Christianity has never yet penetrated. . . . Religion gets its morality from humans. It's a feedback loop.[6]

But Hitchens's insistence that "morality is innate" didn't resolve things for Alex. He wrestled terribly for quite some time.

---

5 Fyodor Dostoevsky, *The Brothers Karamazov*, trans. Richard Pevear and Larissa Volokhonsky (New York: Farrar, Straus and Giroux, 1990), 82, 632.

6 *Collision: Christopher Hitchens vs. Douglas Wilson*, directed by Darren Doane, produced by Crux Pictures/Gorilla Poet Productions (Level4 Studios, 2009), min. 20.

He wondered: *If morality is innate in people, why isn't it innate in all people? If Christopher Hitchens is right for condemning Saddam Hussein, why didn't that innate sense of right and wrong evolve in the many followers of Hussein?* When Hitchens supported the war in Iraq, for what he deemed moral reasons, why hadn't all his secular, liberal, fellow journalists agreed, based on their "innate" sense of right and wrong? Even more disturbing to Alex was the thought that perhaps Hitchens's morality flowed more consistently from a theistic worldview than from an atheist one.

This did more than create intellectual headaches for Alex as he began his freshman year in college. Hitchens's failure to consistently defend his view of ethics triggered panic attacks in Alex, along with sleeplessness and a sense that a foundation was crumbling. Not all spiritual journeys are pleasant—at least, not at every point along the way. But we should not quit climbing just because the terrain poses difficulties.

Social Signposts

Hitchens's arrogance and hypocrisy stood out starkly for Alex as he spent time with some Christians on his campus.

> They were nice to me even though they had no reason to be. I certainly wasn't nice to them! One of my favorite tactics was to insult Christians until they blasted back at me with unkind attacks. Then I'd smile and say, "I guess Jesus is really pleased with you right now." But the Christian guys I met in college didn't fall for that. It didn't work on them. They seemed calm— a dramatic contrast to what I'd seen growing up. These Christians also showed amazing respect for people with whom they

disagreed—a dramatic contrast to what Christopher Hitchens displayed almost all the time.

The complexity of spiritual journeys is due in part to the social environment around us. Like Alex, Hitchens found Christians to be nicer than expected. In an online article titled "Faith No More: What I've Learned from Debating Religious People around the World," he admitted, "The so-called Christian right is much less monolithic, and very much more polite and hospitable, than I would once have thought, or than most liberals believe."[7]

Almost against his better judgement, Alex agreed to discuss the Bible with a few Christians he had come to respect. They focused their investigation on the book of Romans in the New Testament. The first thing Alex noticed was the book's high estimation of nature. In the very first chapter, the argument begins with, "For his invisible attributes, namely, his eternal power and divine nature, have been clearly perceived, ever since the creation of the world, in the things that have been made."[8] Alex loved the outdoors, walking through heavily wooded areas near his home and hiking in the Blue Ridge Mountains. This is where he felt peace, a dramatic contrast to the angst and anger that surrounded him at his religious school. Reading Romans made him wonder if his experiences in the outdoors were closer to what God intended than the nonsense at the indoor religion of his church. This was both comforting and confusing.

---

7   Christopher Hitchens, "Faith No More: What I've Learned from Debating Religious People around the World," October 26, 2009, *Slate*, http://www.slate.com/.

8   Romans 1:20.

Then he came to more pointed teaching in Romans. "I loved the fact that the Bible promised punishment to sinful people. When I read 'on account of this, the wrath of God is coming,'[9] I said, 'Yeah! Those hypocrites at my school deserve to be nuked." The problem was, as Alex let down his guard, he had to admit he *also* might deserve punishment for his own nastiness.

> I wasn't too happy with the verse, "all have sinned and fall short of the glory of God,"[10] but I couldn't totally dismiss it. At the same time, I was struck by the statement that God was both "just and the justifier."[11] God demands payment for sin, but he also provides payment for sin. As I started accepting this idea, I found I was able to sleep—perhaps for the first time in years. And I was no longer angry. I couldn't quite explain it, but I couldn't deny it either.

Alex's and Hitchens's multifaceted stories point to an important observation on our indirect journey of questioning faith:

People approach faith with many motives, not just one.

As multifaceted persons, we don't address complex topics like God, belief, faith, and religion with impartial rationality. Our motives are many, not singular; mixed, not pure; complex, not simple; woven through many aspects of our personhood, not just through logical intellect. We must admit this if we're to make progress in

9 See Romans 1:18.
10 Romans 3:23.
11 Romans 3:26.

firming up important foundational issues of our lives, even if it surfaces things we'd rather not see.

Social psychologists and other researchers have asserted this from numerous angles. They make statements like "Intuitions come first, strategic reasoning second"[12] and "Motivation is a forest full of twisting trees, unexplored rivers, threatening insects, weird plants, and colorful birds."[13] They use phrases like "predictably irrational"[14] and suggest that we have different ways of thinking, some of which are not all that logical.[15]

Somehow, many of us have not considered this as much as we should, particularly when it comes to faith. Thus, both believers and doubters oversimplify their bases for embracing or shunning spiritual considerations.

When writer and philosopher Aldous Huxley reflected on his beliefs, he acknowledged:

> I had motives for not wanting the world to have any meaning; consequently assumed that it had not; and was able without any difficulty to find satisfying reasons for this assumption. . . . For myself . . . the philosophy of meaninglessness was essentially an instrument of liberation, sexual and political.[16]

12 Jonathan Haidt, *The Righteous Mind: Why Good People Are Divided by Politics and Religion* (New York: Pantheon, 2012), 91.
13 Dan Ariely, *Payoff: The Hidden Logic That Shapes Our Motivations* (New York: Simon & Schuster, 2016), 3.
14 Dan Ariely, *Predictably Irrational: The Hidden Forces That Shape Our Decisions* (New York: Harper Perennial, 2010).
15 See, for example, Daniel Kahneman, *Thinking Fast and Slow* (New York: Farrar, Straus and Giroux, 2011).
16 Aldous Huxley, *Ends and Means* (London: Chatto & Windus, 1941), 272.

More succinctly and more recently, philosophy professor Thomas Nagel has written: "It isn't just that I don't believe in God and, naturally, hope that I'm right in my belief. It's that I hope there is no God! I don't want there to be a God; I don't want the universe to be like that."[17]

To be fair, I must point out that mixed motives can push people toward religion as well as away from it. Edward Gibbon, the English historian, acknowledged that his conversion to Roman Catholicism years earlier was "provoked by theological arguments, but it was undoubtedly also an act of rebellion against his father." Leo Damrosch, professor of literature at Harvard, concluded that "a few years later [James] Boswell would do the same thing."[18]

Honest Introspection

The thread of anger ties Alex's and Christopher's journeys together. You felt it while reading their accounts, didn't you? I saw it on Alex's face as he sat across from me at a coffee shop remembering emotions as well as ideas. But his whole demeanor changed when he shared the next section of his path. His times with his new friends felt like a confluence of rivers—stimulating ideas from the book of Romans, deepening appreciation for the beauty of nature, laughter with friends instead of anger, and—best of all—dramatically better sleep. Somewhere amid all that, Alex became a Christian. I realize that last sentence needs a lot of clarification. We'll explore that further in the chapters ahead.

---

17 Thomas Nagel, *The Last Word* (New York: Oxford University Press, 2001), 130.
18 Leo Damrosch, *The Club: Johnson, Boswell, and the Friends Who Shaped an Age* (New Haven, CT: Yale University Press, 2019), 325n6; and Edward Gibbon, *Memoirs of My Life*, ed. Georges A. Bonnard (London: Nelson, 1966), 56–61.

For now, it's worth considering one more segment of Alex's journey. Several years later, when he learned of Hitchens's diagnosis of stage 4 cancer, he wrote his former hero a letter, encouraging him to reconsider faith. "Mostly, I was writing him to thank him. Ironically, Hitchens may have been the most influential person in my Christian conversion. But I never heard back from him."

After one public debate, a camera caught Hitchens in an un-guarded moment when he recalled a conversation with Richard Dawkins. The fellow atheist had posed the idea of wiping out all religion through debate and reason. Hitchens shared:

> At one point, if I could convert everyone in the world, not convert but convince, to be a non-believer and I'd really done brilliantly, and there's only one left. One more, and then it'd be done. There'd be no more religion in the world. No more deism, theism. I wouldn't do it.
>
> And Dawkins said, "What do you mean you wouldn't do it?" I said, "I don't quite know why I wouldn't do it." And it's not just because there'd be nothing left to argue with, and no one left to argue with. It's not just that. Though it would be that. Somehow if I could drive it out of the world, I wouldn't. And the incredulity with which he [Dawkins] looked at me, stays with me still, I've got to say.[19]

As we continue to question faith in the chapters ahead, ask yourself if you're approaching faith with a mix of motives. Are

19 *Collision: Christopher Hitchens vs. Douglas Wilson*, 1:24:15.

you willing to raise the question of whether you're even aware of all your motivations? You may not realize all that's going on inside you as you encounter claims or arguments or clues about realms outside your everyday life. You might not see clearly the path you're on until you reach a higher vantage point and turn around. But it may still be worth the journey—even if the terrain seems a bit daunting.

2

The Question of Trust

What If Faith Is Inevitable, Not Optional?

WHEN KENYON COLLEGE invited David Foster Wallace to speak at their 2005 commencement, they knew they had a winner. His category-defying novel *Infinite Jest* continued to sell well, despite being nearly ten years old. As a professor, he had credibility within academia. As an entertaining writer, he would connect well with students. He was hailed as the voice of a generation. *Infinite Jest* incarnated many of postmodernism's philosophical assertions but expressed them through a pop-culture-esque, sometimes absurd series of disjointed sketches.

What Kenyon College didn't anticipate was that Wallace had morphed into someone who "differed at this point almost 180 degrees from the Wallace of popular imagination; . . . [he had become] an intense moralist . . . an apostle of careful living and hard work," his biographer, D. T. Max, observed.[1]

---

1   D. T. Max, *Every Love Story Is a Ghost Story: A Life of David Foster Wallace* (New York: Penguin, 2013), 284.

Wallace delivered his words in his academic robe, bent slightly forward, a lock of hair covering his face, sweat dripping down his neck, in his intense, slightly quavering voice, speaking modestly and hesitantly. It was as if there was nothing more uncomfortable for him than being there, at this podium, but what he had to say was too important to keep it to himself.[2]

His speech, later published as a separate short book entitled *This Is Water*, reached its zenith with words that have since been quoted widely. They hit like a fiery preacher's sermon:

In the day-to-day trenches of adult life, there is actually no such thing as atheism. There is no such thing as not worshipping. Everybody worships. The only choice we get is *what* to worship. And an outstanding reason for choosing some sort of god or spiritual-type thing to worship—be it J.C. or Allah, be it Yahweh or the Wiccan mother-goddess or the Four Noble Truths or some infrangible set of ethical principles—is that pretty much anything else you worship will eat you alive. If you worship money and things—if they are where you tap real meaning in life—then you will never have enough. Never feel you have enough. It's the truth. Worship your own body and beauty and sexual allure and you will always feel ugly, and when time and age start showing, you will die a million deaths before they finally plant you. On one level we all know this stuff already—it's been codified as myths, proverbs, clichés, bromides, epigrams, parables; the skeleton of every great story. The trick is keeping the truth up front in daily

2   Max, *Every Love Story*, 286.

consciousness. Worship power—you will feel weak and afraid, and you will need ever more power over others to keep the fear at bay. Worship your intellect, being seen as smart—you will end up feeling stupid, a fraud, always on the verge of being found out.[3]

He continued:

Look, the insidious thing about these forms of worship is not that they're evil or sinful. It is that they are unconscious. They are default settings. They are the kind of worship you just gradually slip into, day after day, getting more and more selective about what you see and how you measure value without ever being fully aware that that's what you're doing.[4]

This chapter explores whether Wallace was right. Does everyone worship? Put another way, is faith inevitable? Do we all trust in something that gives us meaning, purpose, an identity, or a lens through which to view our lives and the world around us? And, as Wallace states so disturbingly, are some "gods" not worthy of our allegiance? Do some objects of worship "eat us alive"?

A Common Object of Worship

That seemed to be the case for Georgiana. She told me acceptance was her object of worship. Acceptance from men is what she

---

3 David Foster Wallace, *This Is Water: Some Thoughts, Delivered on a Significant Occasion, about Living a Compassionate Life* (New York: Little, Brown, 2009), 98–111, emphasis original.

4 These four sentences were not included in the book but can be heard on numerous audio recordings of Wallace's address. See David Foster Wallace, "This Is Water," 2005 commencement speech at Kenyon College, https://www.youtube.com/.

craved. "That's why I threw myself at pretty much every frat guy I met in my first semester of college," she shared. "I built my core identity around men. I put so much of my worth in relationships. If I had a boyfriend, I felt okay about myself. If I didn't have one, I felt empty."

We met at a crowded coffee shop, and I was struck by how freely Georgiana told me difficult details from her life. She was born one year after her parents got married, and one year after that her parents got divorced. She was raised by her mother, whom she described as a serial dater. "There was always another new guy in our house. They'd move in with us or we'd move in with them. We moved around a lot."

She also said she felt a lot of pressure from both her parents to perform to a high standard of excellence. Her mother was concerned about how well Georgiana did in school, and her father told her how embarrassed he'd be in front of his friends if she didn't get into a top-tier college. Her mother also stressed how important it was to look good, dress well, and always present a good image. "I always had to meet my parents' expectations. It was like, 'You have to have good grades to make Mom happy, to make me proud of you.' I was always feeling like I had to do these things to have my mom accept me for who I am."

The reason Georgiana and I were meeting was so she could tell me her story of coming to faith as a Christian. But for the first half hour of our conversation, that part of the story seemed unlikely and a long way off. "I never understood anything about Christianity when I was growing up. Both my parents were turned off by religion, and the only impressions I got of Christians were from the media, you know, like crazy Christian pastors yelling at people."

By the time she got to college, she identified herself as an atheist and felt no need to explore anything about God in any way. But things started changing after she broke up with her boyfriend right at the start of her freshman year in college. They'd been dating for several years through high school, but at some point she felt "degraded" by him because of the way he treated her sexually.

"Sex always had to be a part of a dating relationship for me— just like my mother modeled with her relationships. That just seemed normal and expected. If you were dating someone, you were having sex with him." But then I noticed her facial expression change for the first time in our coffee shop conversation. She told me that a lot of those men her mother dated were abusive toward her. She used the term "sexual trauma" several times in reference to her mother's boyfriends as well as her high school boyfriend. "I didn't realize it at the time, but they were using me in pretty horrible ways."

So, without a boyfriend, she went to a lot of parties, hoping to find a new guy for her affections. On the outside, she seemed happy. But internally,

> I did a lot of really bad things and felt empty inside. I was turning into my mom! I was anxious. Everything I thought would bring me happiness or answers didn't work. My life was leading to nothing. I remember thinking, "This is my life, and I don't like it."

By December of that year—after less than one semester—Georgiana didn't want to live. "I never made a plan to end my life, but I ideated about suicide all the time. And people who lived on my dorm floor could tell something was wrong. I wasn't my bubbly, outgoing self anymore."

One night, she got into a long conversation with a guy who lived in her dorm, and she found herself thinking about life in a different way than she had been thinking all semester. He was a Christian, but their conversation really wasn't that much about God or religion. She wouldn't have stuck around for that, because of her negative views of Christians. She thought they were a bunch of weird, stupid fanatics. But the conversation with this guy was about life and happiness on a much larger scale and "was deeper than any conversation I had with any of my friends."

He invited her to a meeting of a Christian organization on campus, and she said she'd go, but "I only went because this guy was cute, and I wanted to sit next to him at the meeting. But as soon as we walked in the door, he left me to go hang out with his friends."

At this point, she started speaking a lot faster.

> It was so awkward. I sat way in the back and didn't talk to anyone. It was also weird. They sang songs for a really long time, and I couldn't relate to these people. The only thing I knew about Jesus was that Christmas was supposedly his birthday. Then the speaker got up and talked for a long time. I had no clue what he was talking about.

She paused and looked up at me more directly, then continued, speaking more slowly.

> I don't remember the topic the speaker was talking about, but I'll never forget his passion. He was so passionate about Jesus.

I don't think I ever heard anyone talk so passionately about *anything*. And he was talking about Jesus like he was right there next to him on the stage. I remember thinking, *I don't know why but I'm definitely coming back to this group.*

It wasn't a smooth ride after that. She came to only one more meeting that semester and inconsistently for several months the next semester. Then she started going to a Bible study, where she was sure she was the only non-Christian in the room. She also got into yet another sexually degrading relationship with a guy that left her feeling like she was living a double life. But the contrast helped clarify things. From the guy, it was all conditional love—just like she experienced from all those other guys, as well as her parents. And it was abusive. But from the women in the Bible study, especially Karen, the leader, it was "kindness, patience, and, unconditional love."

"Usually, I'm quiet and introverted, but I was the most talkative person in that Bible study," she went on. "I started meeting with Karen one-on-one. Part of that was because I just didn't want the other women in the study to hear all my questions. But part of it was more than just intellectual. Over time, I was just getting enamored with Jesus." At this point she laughed and said: "I can't believe how patient Karen was with me. And she never checked her phone when we met. That meant a lot to me. I was her total focus."

Toward the end of that spring semester, Georgiana told Karen she was ready to become a Christian.

In that conversation, it all came together for me. I started tearing up. Because of my past, my upbringing, I only knew love that was conditional, and that kind of love is so fragile. But God loves people who are sinful like me! That's what I was searching for with all those guys and all those parties. Now I know why those other things weren't making me happy.

Georgiana told me she closed her eyes and prayed to tell God she wanted to become a Christian, that she finally understood why Jesus had to die to pay for her sins. "When I finished praying, the first thing Karen said to me was: 'Oh, I'm so sorry. There are so many people around us. I should have picked a more private spot.' But I told her I didn't care." For someone usually concerned about what others thought of her, that observation stood out to me.

I asked her to elaborate a bit on what she meant when she said she was enamored with Jesus. Here's what she told me:

I meant there were encounters people had with Jesus that were just amazing. Especially his interactions with women. Women like the woman at the well[5] or the woman caught in adultery,[6] where Jesus gave grace to women who suffered from sexual sin like I did. That became so important to me that I was beginning to understand that Jesus didn't have limits to his grace, that there wasn't an extent to what he could forgive or save us from. I was also enamored by the fact that God wanted to be so closely associated with us, that he took on human form, and that he readily sacrificed himself for humanity, that he is there waiting to take the shame that was plaguing my sense of identity

5 John 4:1–26.
6 John 8:1–11.

and worth. It was easy for me to see myself as sinful, but so much more to understand how Jesus came for sinners like me.

Acceptance from men had been Georgiana's default god. She decided to take a full year off from dating anyone, just to get free from depending on a relationship with a guy. That strategy worked. When she started dating a Christian guy over a year later, that relationship felt totally different from all her previous ones. As we left the coffee shop, she showed me a photo from her wedding. She and her husband exchanged their vows outdoors, under umbrellas. "It poured that day. But we didn't care."

Identity as Idol

The theme of setting your affections, dependence, or identity on an idolized desire surfaced in conversations I had with others as well. As with Georgiana, the idols ate people alive. Take Thomas for instance. He also craved acceptance and affection. And like her, he desired it from men. Once Thomas quit denying his desires and accepted he was gay, he found no shortage of men to sleep with. With each liaison, he hoped he'd find the security and love of a lifelong partner.

Thomas felt no need to reconcile his sexuality with the Christian faith of his upbringing. He'd met quite a few Christians who resorted to a unique vocabulary and louder volume whenever they spoke about the LGBT+ community. Thomas vividly remembers attending a Christian campus fellowship as an undergraduate where the speaker railed against the sinfulness of homosexuality. The longer the speaker's tirade, the firmer Thomas's conviction: "This is not a safe place for me."

"They didn't understand," he told me years after that painful meeting.

They didn't *want* to understand. They weren't even trying to understand. They didn't want to hear that people don't "choose" to be gay. I certainly hadn't. I felt gay as early as seven or eight years old. For many Christians, it's a simple black and white issue. But sexuality is never that simplistic.

So, after graduating from college and landing a job as a music teacher, Thomas came out, and he finally found the affirmation he was looking for. The worlds of music and education had long affirmed sexual variety as natural. Thomas's peers spoke freely about a gay "identity." And that term galvanized Thomas's view of himself. He was gay. That was his primary identity, and it would never change. No one challenged Thomas on that assumption for many years.

But then Thomas dared to come out to a longtime Christian friend, Nathan. Thomas expected Nathan to reject him. He anticipated another ranting lecture like the one he heard at the Christian fellowship. But Nathan surprised him. Nathan fit in neither the condemnation nor the affirmation camp. Instead, he thanked Thomas for telling him something so personal, and he expressed gratitude for Thomas's friendship. Nathan hoped this moment wouldn't change the fact that they were friends. But then Nathan expressed something Thomas had never heard before, a concern that homosexuality might not be good.

"I realize you may think this is natural. But what feels natural may not be good." Nathan asked Thomas if he'd ever heard that people's sexual desires can sometimes change. Thomas wanted to throw up. Outwardly, he stayed in the conversation, but inwardly, he knew this was the end of that friendship.

A few weeks later, Nathan sent Thomas a book, Joe Dallas's *Desires in Conflict*, the honest account of a man who felt a spiritual draw toward Christianity and a sexual allure toward men. Thomas threw the book against the wall. He cursed Nathan out loud and tried to forget all about the book. Oddly, Thomas didn't throw it in the trash. Over time, he began to read parts of the book and had to admit there was some truth in it.

Dallas recounted how he'd been sexually abused by an older man when he was young, and he admitted that while horrible, it did provide a form of affirmation and affection. This resonated with Thomas. He too had been sexually abused—many times over, by numerous men. He too found it affirming, albeit perversely so. "It was a way to get attention," he shared with me. But reading that book (and then several more) shed light on unexplored parts of his past. Thomas had to admit that his relationships with both men and women had long been unhealthy. He had to acknowledge that his view of God and Christianity was distorted as well.

Reading the book was the start of a long exploration of his beliefs, desires, and affections. It took several years, lots of counseling, and involvement in support groups, but Thomas began to feel healthy in ways he hadn't in a very long time. He started to question whether sexuality is a valid basis for one's identity. He needed something more transcendent for that category. He also saw how unhealthy it was to seek validation from men. This explained why so many of his gay partnerships ended so badly, and with such devastating explosions of anger. "My anger showed me that I was demanding too much from men. I was trying to fill a bottomless pit, and I needed to sort out my thinking before I could relate to people in a healthier way."

The process was far from easy. Thomas began attending a church where people heard his story, accepted him for who he was, but did *not* affirm his sinful behavior. This reminded Thomas of the story in the Bible where Jesus told the woman caught in adultery, "Neither do I condemn you," but then added, "go, and from now on sin no more."[7] No condemning. No condoning. Thomas also heard stories from others in the church who struggled with sin. "We're all sinners, and we all need a Savior," they told him.

Years later, as a member of a singles' group at his church, Thomas found himself attracted to some of the women. Some may find this surprising (or think it impossible), but Thomas told me that sexual attraction is rarely as one-dimensional as our culture likes to advertise.[8] More to the point, if we all followed our desires, we'd destroy all relationships. Faithful heterosexual monogamy has never been easy or felt natural, but it's good. The alternatives have left countless people damaged and lonely, all in the name of authentic expression of their sexual identity.

Thomas eventually married a woman from that church, but he doesn't speak about it as simplistic or as merely choosing heterosexuality over homosexuality. It's far more complex and related to redefining his identity as one who has God as his ultimate object of worship, a higher priority than pleasure, affirmation, or self-expression.

7 John 8:11.
8 Rebecca McLaughlin, *The Secular Creed: Engaging Five Contemporary Claims* (Austin, TX: Gospel Coalition, 2021), 54.

A Variety of Religious Experiences

Austin told me his god was control. He was obsessed with controlling what he ate, how perfectly he kept to his exercise regimen, who was in charge of every conversation and every relationship, and what he chose to do with his body sexually. But he admitted that all this just made him a very mean, angry guy. Control is a tough deity to satisfy.

If faith is inevitable and everyone worships, it may be that some objects of worship aren't monumental. Connie told me that drinking and competitive softball were "basically what my husband's life and mine were all about." They lived for the weekend, when the alcohol flowed freely, and the softball tournaments played center stage. It was fun while it lasted, but looking back decades later, Connie said it didn't last all that long. The softball fun couldn't carry the difficult realities of her life, like the death of a close friend and the collapse of her marriage.

A case can be made that worship was also at the center of David Crosby's life. Though he probably wouldn't have used that term, one may wonder why he kept touring, composing, singing, and performing well into his seventies. Crosby, Stills, and Nash—and, later, Young—became one of the most successful rock groups of all time. Some thought they would overtake the Beatles in popularity in the late 1960s and '70s. At David's age of almost eighty, his health and voice made the on-the-road-again life unwise, probably unnecessary (some estimate his net worth to be over $40 million), and unwanted by his wife, Jan.

"I don't think people know how sick he really is," Jan told an interviewer in the documentary about David's life, *Remember My*

Name, released just a few years before he died. But she continued that if she were to say to him, "Hey, honey, I think you should stay here and go see the heart people right now . . . he would say, '[expletive] you' and walk out the door."[9] *Remember My Name* includes many admissions of regret on Crosby's part. In fact, in just the first few minutes, he admits: "People ask me if I got regrets. Yeah, I got a huge regret about the time I wasted being smashed. I'm afraid. I'm afraid of dying. And I'm close. And I don't like it. I'd like to have more time—a lot more time."

> INTERVIEWER. If I could come to you and say, "No music," but you could have extreme joy in your home life, incredible family . . . no music. Do you make that trade?
>
> CROSBY. No. That's not a world for me.
>
> INTERVIEWER. And is that a selfish thing?
>
> CROSBY. I don't know. Maybe. No music? No. I'm not interested. It's the only thing I can contribute, the only thing I got to offer.

Toward the end of the film, he raises the volume of his voice and the intensity of his delivery with these summarizing words: "The one thing I can do is make music. Myself. So, I'm trying really hard to do that." His interviewer asks, "To prove to yourself . . . ?" Crosby responds, "That I'm worth a [expletive]."

If worship includes engaging in an activity to gain an identity or meaning or purpose or validation of worth, it seems that Crosby's life fits the definition well. He's not alone.

---

9   These quotes and all of David's come from the documentary *David Crosby: Remember My Name*, directed by A. J. Eaton, produced by Cameron Crowe (BMG, 2019).

Our Worship-Filled World

It might be, in our so-called secular age, when more and more people check the box labeled "none" (see p. *4*) on surveys and drop-down menus about religion, that we've simply found other things to become religious about.

Tara Isabella Burton certainly believes this to be so. In her carefully researched book *Strange Rites: New Religions for a Godless World*, she argues that a dramatically increasing number of trends propel people to dedicate their time, money, and devotion to a wide array of objects in ways that rival the most ardent of religious adherents.

> If you've ever been to a yoga studio or a CrossFit class, ever practiced "self-care" with a ten-step Korean beauty routine or a Gwyneth Paltrow–sanctioned juice cleanse, ever written or read Internet fan fiction, ever compared your spiritual outlook to a Dungeons and Dragons classification ("lawful good, chaotic evil") or your personal temperament to that of a Hogwarts house, ever channeled your sense of cosmic purpose into social justice activism, ever tried to "bio-hack" yourself or used a meditation app like Headspace, ever negotiated "personals relationship rules"—be they kink or ethical nonmonogamy—with a partner, ever cleansed a house with sage, or ever been wary of a person's "toxic energy," you've participated in some of these trends. There are more.[10]

For a while, many people used the phrase "spiritual but not religious" to describe their faith preference. Some of those people

---

10 Tara Isabella Burton, *Strange Rites: New Religions for a Godless World* (New York: Hachette, 2020), 10–11.

were neither religious nor spiritual but found the phrase helpful for freedom to pursue hedonistic pleasures. But Burton shows that many people who use the phrase today really *are* spiritual but not in an "organized religion" way. They find a sense of transcendence, community, and meaning in their online worlds of Harry Potter fandom or mindfulness training videos or faithful following of TikTok gurus. Burton calls them "religiously Remixed." But make no mistake, people today are more religious than ever, and "we may not all be Remixed, but we all live in a Remixed nation."[11]

Insightfully, she observes, "Scholars of religion often claim that it's impossible to separate out the invention of the printing press from the Protestant Reformation. . . . The Remixed religions . . . are the religions of the Internet."[12] Just as the printing press gave people the ability to read texts for themselves in the privacy of their homes, the Internet facilitates a self-curated, eclectic set of beliefs, values, and practices, and it enables (encourages!) people to be their own priests, rabbis, or ministers and design deities to their own specifications.

Burton does not present herself as a religious zealot, scolding her contemporaries for pursuing gods that cannot satisfy. She begins her book with an honest and vulnerable account of her own almost cultlike devotion to the immersive, experiential play *Sleep No More*, a "near-wordless, dance-based, Hitchcock-inflected retelling of *Macbeth*."[13] She became a fanatic, experiencing the show more than a dozen times, which is nothing compared to many others who see it "ten, twenty, fifty, one hundred times—spending

11 Burton, *Strange Rites*, 25.
12 Burton, *Strange Rites*, 11.
13 Burton, *Strange Rites*, 3.

about $100 a ticket."[14] She tells of one couple who did nothing else for "entertainment" for several years (spending over seventeen thousand dollars in the process) because, as the wife told Burton, "every time I come out [at the end of the experience] I break into the biggest smile. It feels like I've come home." Burton says that for her and for many others, *Sleep No More* was "a home. And therapy session. And a bordello. And, yes, a church."[15] She even says her experiences were part of her journey "to faith—but that's a story for a different book."[16]

After exploring these many "new religions for a godless world," she concludes: "We do not live in a godless world. Rather, we live in a profoundly anti-institutional one. . . . America is not secular but simply spiritually self-focused."[17]

Work as Worship

For many, perhaps our jobs have become our religion. Carolyn Chen, in her book *Work Pray Code: When Work Becomes Religion in Silicon Valley* seems to think so. She believes the workplace has become the center of most everything in a lot of people's lives. The "office" is not just where they work. It's also where they eat their employer-provided, free, gourmet meals; work out at the onsite gym; unwind at employer-sponsored yoga classes; get health care at the onsite clinic; and find, sooner or later, that, given how their job affords them an identity and meaning, their so-called workplace might really be their de facto house of worship.

---

14 Burton, *Strange Rites*, 4.
15 Burton, *Strange Rites*, 5.
16 Burton, *Strange Rites*, 13.
17 Burton, *Strange Rites*, 242.

She calls this all-consuming environment "Techtopia," saying this is

> where people find their highest fulfillment in the utopian work-place. It promises high-skilled Americans a new kind of "whole-ness." Professionally managed, data-driven, meritocratic, and designed to scale, Techtopia gives tech workers what their families, religions, neighborhoods, unions, and civic organizations have failed to deliver in the last forty years: meaning, purpose, recogni-tion, spirituality, and community. It is the twenty-first century American Dream.[18]

But does Techtopia really deliver meaning? Can it fulfill souls while it fills schedules? More and more people are staying in the workforce longer and later in their lives. In Derek Thompson's *Atlantic* article "Why the Old Elite Spend So Much Time at Work," he writes, "Some 70- and 80-somethings loving their work so much that they never retire is awfully close to something I've called *workism*—the idea that work has, for many elites, become a kind of personal religion in an era of otherwise declining religiosity."[19]

For others, politics is the new religion—with some pretty ugly displays of worshipful fervor. "This is what religion without religion looks like," writes Shadi Hamid, showing how both the leftward progressives and the rightward nationalists display remarkable levels of self-righteousness, presumptuousness, and

18 Carolyn Chen, *Work Pray Code: When Work Becomes Religion in Silicon Valley* (Prince-ton, NJ: Princeton University Press, 2022), 196.

19 Derek Thompson, "Why the Old Elite Spend So Much Time at Work," *Atlantic*, August 3, 2022, https://www.theatlantic.com/.

the harshest of condemnations for all who disagree. He asks and answers:

> Can religiosity be effectively channeled into political belief without the structures of actual religion to temper and postpone judgment? There is little sign, so far, that it can. If matters of good and evil are not to be resolved by an omniscient God in the future, then America will judge and render punishment now. We are a nation of believers.[20]

On our journey of questioning faith, we arrive at another important turn in the road. We must consider seriously that everyone has faith, not just so-called religious people or those who say they're "spiritual but not religious." In other words, we need to grapple with this observation:

Faith is inevitable, not optional.

Second Things Second

At this point, I must make an important qualification. Many of the things people set their affections on or build their identities on or worship aren't necessarily bad things (though certainly some are). Intimacy in relationships, good health through exercise, perfecting a craft or an art, pursuing a career, valuing family, and a thousand other things are not bad things at all. They're just not ultimate things. They're good gifts but lousy gods. Both Georgiana and David Foster Wallace (as we'll discover below) had legitimate reasons for

20 Shadi Hamid, "America without God," in *Atlantic*, April 2021, https://www.the atlantic.com/.

wanting the kind of connectedness you can have through romantic relationships. We're wired for connection. But when we demand more from those relationships than they can provide (a source of identity, a foundation for worth, a sense of meaning or purpose, etc.), we set ourselves up for disappointment (at the very least) or, far worse, getting "eaten alive" with crushing despair.

C. S. Lewis (we'll hear more about him in later chapters) found this to be true in his journey from atheism to faith. He loved literature and mythology but found them an insufficient foundation for all his life and affections. He wrote, "You can't get second things by putting them first; you can get second things only by putting first things first."[21] In another place, he concluded, "Put first things first and we get second things thrown in; put second things first and we lose both first and second things."[22]

Choosing Our Gods Carefully

When we circle back to consider David Foster Wallace's advice that we choose carefully what we worship, it serves us well to ask how well he followed this advice. Tragically, it seems he didn't do well in that department. He got "eaten alive" by his worship of admiration and acceptance, along with demands for loyalty from other people, especially women.

Adrienne Miller, with whom he developed a long-term relationship, spoke of his obsession for control, a seemingly bottomless need for affirmation, and demands for secrecy and protection of

---

21 C. S. Lewis, "First and Second Things," in *God in the Dock* (Grand Rapids, MI: Eerdmans, 1970), 278–80.
22 *The Collected Letters of C. S. Lewis*, vol. 3, *Narnia, Cambridge, and Joy, 1950–1963*, ed. Walter Hooper (San Francisco: HarperSanFrancisco, 2007), 111.

privacy.[23] She also recounted numerous outbursts of rage when she failed to obey him.

Not far below the surface, according to Wallace's biographer, D. T. Max, lay an insecurity and self-loathing that never adequately found relief. Max summarized it this way:

> Wallace never felt safe disclosing himself. He worried, then as he always would later, that to know him too well would be to dislike him. Or at least dislike him as much as he disliked himself. He felt a fake, a victim, as he would later write, of "imposter syndrome."[24]

Wallace was obsessed with sex, sleeping with countless women, preferring, as he wrote to a friend, "serial high-romance and low-intimacy" relationships. He craved an intimacy those fleeting experiences could not provide and, in all probability, exacerbated his problem and conviction that "no one likes me."[25]

By the time Wallace stepped to the podium to deliver his Kenyon College address, he had learned some transformational, sobering lessons through therapy, AA support group meetings, and the stability of a marriage to Karen Green. Thus, his preachy tone and modernist moralism differed dramatically from his postmodern meanderings in *Infinite Jest*. But the fact that he committed suicide just three years after Kenyon shows how incomplete his recovery was.

23 See Adrienne Miller, *In the Land of Men: A Memoir* (New York: HarperCollins, 2020), 222.

24 Max, *Every Love Story*, 8.

25 Miller, *In the Land of Men*, 326.

To be sure, Wallace's mental illness was complex. Some of it may have stemmed from chemical imbalance that numerous medications never quite conquered. But to chalk up his suicide solely to limits of pharmacology (or his decision to stop or reduce his medication) fails to consider the complexity of depression and, more significantly, of human makeup and experience. As we saw in the previous chapter, we are multifaceted creatures. We accept reductionist views of who we are to our own peril.

Questioning the Objects of Faith

At this point, I'm saying that we all have faith. It's just a matter of discerning the object of our faith. A little introspection about this can go a long way. Where have you placed your most significant hopes? On what have you built your identity? How intentional were you in latching your allegiances to these objects? And how has your faith shaped you? Pause a bit and reflect before starting the next chapter.

3

The Question of Confidence

What If Absolute Certainty Isn't Necessary?

I SPEND ENTIRELY TOO MUCH time (and money!) at the Apple store. At one point, I wondered if I was on a first-name basis with every "genius" and "expert" who worked there. When I was about to begin a doctoral program that would require a lot of writing and research, I ventured in to purchase a new MacBook Pro. My Apple expert, Cory, helped me determine the precise number of megahertz and megabytes I would need and started the ordering process. While we waited for my computer to emerge, he made small talk about what kind of doctorate I was about to pursue.

"It's in intercultural studies," I responded.

"Ooh. Fascinating," he said, sounding more interested than just the typical salesman offering chitchat. "What aspects of culture are you interested in studying?"

"Mostly religion," I said. "I want to see how different belief systems compare and interact with each other."

In similar situations, my conversation partners have responded with a polite "Oh, that's interesting" and changed the topic. I wondered if Cory would drop the topic.

"I used to be religious," he said. "Christian."

"What happened?" I asked.

"I had too many doubts. I just couldn't be 100 percent sure."

"Oh, I've never been 100 percent sure," I said.

"Wait! What?"

"I'd say, most of the time, I'm in the mid-90s when it comes to how sure I am of my faith. When terrible things happen, I dip lower. But I'm never at 100."

"But you said you're going for a doctorate in this stuff."

"Oh! That might make things even worse."

I paused to see if he was following. He was.

"Look," I explained, "I just think absolute certainty is beyond my brain level. I'm going for a doctorate. But I'm not a genius (and I'm not talking about the people who work in the back of your store). In fact, I think absolute certainty is beyond *anyone's* brain level. I think that kind of hubris might have come more from the Enlightenment than from the Bible. I think the Bible offers a high level of confidence. But not absolute certainty."

Just then, Cory's phone buzzed, letting us both know my computer was ready. He had to tend to other customers. But he thanked me and told me I gave him something to think about.

What do you think? Do you need absolute certainty to believe something? Some skeptics tell me that even the slightest bit of doubt rules out religious faith. They often tell me that science is a much better way to know things and that, through science, we can have certainty.

But that's not what I've heard from scientists.

For seventeen years, I had the privilege of facilitating a discussion group of university professors who also happened to be Christians. They came from a variety of academic disciplines, more than half of them in the physical sciences. Different individuals took turns presenting papers about the intersections of their faith and their field. A frequent refrain included "surprises" they found as they researched medicine, mathematics, chemistry, and physics. Good research, they often commented, revealed as much of what we *don't* know as what we *do* know. Scientists freely admit how much more we still need to find out. We heard echoes of the same reality in history, sociology, psychology, philosophy, and anthropology.

On one occasion, we invited an atheist from the philosophy department to share about his research on religion from a skeptic's perspective. He graciously admitted that all perspectives, from the most convinced atheist to the most ardent Christian, have some level of belief that cannot be proved scientifically or logically. We all live with a gap between what we believe with confidence and what we assume with a "leap of faith." (He used that expression voluntarily.) No one has absolute certainty in his or her beliefs. Confidence seems to be a more realistic goal than certainty.

Christof Koch, a neurophysiologist and the chief scientist of the MindScope Program and former professor at the California Institute of Technology has a faith journey that includes some of the ideas I've mentioned so far. His story moves from a Roman Catholic upbringing to atheist conviction. Somewhere on the route to a PhD at the Max Planck Institute for biological cybernetics, he found the tensions between science and faith too much to reconcile and landed on the side of skepticism.

His academic focus has been on consciousness and its relationship to meaning. He contends that all living creatures have some level of consciousness, and despite humans' naturalistic, evolutionary roots, we still cling to the idea that life has meaning. In his book *Consciousness: Confessions of a Romantic Reductionist*, he admits: "I lost my childhood faith, yet I've never lost my abiding faith that everything is as it should be. I feel deep in my bones that the universe has meaning that we can realize."[1] Note his use of the word "faith." Also note his nonscientific basis for his belief—a feeling deep in his bones. Even a brilliant scientist such as Koch acknowledges the reality of doubt: "I continue to be amazed by the ability of highly educated and intelligent people to fool themselves. . . . Nobody is immune from self-deception and self-delusion."[2] His book is filled with admissions of doubt, because of science's limitations, interspersed with a high level of confidence in the abilities of science to explain the mysteries of life. At best, one can hope he's right in saying we can realize the meaning of things. At worst, a reader might wonder if Koch, himself, is guilty of "self-deception and self-delusion."

Atheists' Doubts

I heard a similar insight—that we all live with a mix of belief and doubt—during a long conversation with Neal, a regional leader of a national atheists' organization. "Anyone who doesn't admit some level of agnosticism is just not being honest," he told me. He recounted how he shifted from a conservative Christian

---

1 Christof Koch, *Consciousness: Confessions of a Romantic Reductionist* (Cambridge, MA: MIT Press, 2017), 12.

2 Koch, *Consciousness*, 158.

upbringing to a skeptical atheist perspective before the age of twenty. His family attended several different Christian churches and never missed a Sunday. "It wasn't optional to skip church. My mother insisted we go every time the church had any kind of event." But as he started reading the Bible for himself, he found too many stories that didn't make sense. How could Jonah live inside a whale? Why did God send bears to kill some teenagers who made fun of Elijah?[3] "It just didn't make sense to me" was a phrase he repeated at least a half dozen times in our hour-long conversation. He also said all the intellectual arguments he heard for the existence of God "left me unsatisfied. If God exists, he gave us reason for a reason." I countered with, "But aren't there limits to human reason?" He quickly agreed.

I tried to point out what seemed like a contradiction to me. He admitted that human reason is limited but rejected things that didn't satisfy his human reason. I don't think he saw my point. As a voracious reader, Neal filled his early years reading encyclopedias, mythology, and books about science. The religious point of view made less and less sense as he read more and more. But Neal freely admitted he could be wrong and has doubts. At several points in our discussion, I shared that all people must deal with some level of uncertainty. He jumped in with "of course," and "I totally agree."

Our time together was enjoyable for us both. We made each other laugh as we challenged each other's assumptions and strongly held beliefs. Three moments stand out to me from our time together as I reflect on our conversation. Early on he shared: "The times that I feel the closest to religious are the times when I feel

3   See Jonah 1:17 and 2 Kings 2:23–25. Note that the biblical story is about Elisha, not Elijah.

a lot of love or support from people I care about. I describe it as feeling blessed because 'lucky' just doesn't feel appropriate."

The second moment elaborates on that prior one. "I feel moments when I feel so fortunate, it can't just be happenstance or circumstance." He paused and then added, "But I accept that it is."

I clarified, "that it is just happenstance?" He nodded yes.

The third highlight came after our lengthy discussion about debates between atheists and Christians he'd watched on YouTube and other websites. I've watched and even sponsored some of these but have always felt disappointed by them. Neal agreed and shared my disappointment. I said my problem was that the debaters rarely did a good job. I told him I felt embarrassed sometimes when Christians really didn't present the religious case very well. And he said he felt the same way about a lot of the atheists! But then he surprised me with this:

> If anything's going to convince me, it's not going to be one of the logical arguments I've heard for God. Not because they're not convincing or not because logical arguments aren't convincing. They're all very unsatisfying. It would have to be God making himself known in some way that's convincing, some sort of personal experience or experiences.

Believers' Doubts

Barry's story is the flip side of Neal's. Raised by unreligious parents, Barry viewed life through a very rational lens. He studied mathematics and science in his undergraduate days and earned a master's degree in engineering. In his twenties, he read Richard Dawkins's *The God Delusion* and found all the Oxford atheist's arguments and conclusions resonated with him. Dawkins gave Barry intellectual support for atheism and helped him grow in boldness about it. "I basically sopped up all of Dawkins, and whenever I got together with friends and the topic of religion came up, I was vocal. I was the atheist in the group, and I was owning the atheist label." The label stuck for a full decade.

That chapter of his life included some losses that he described as traumatic. His wife left him, and his father died. The loss of his father was particularly painful because, from diagnosis to death, it all happened in less than nine months. Speaking at his father's funeral was particularly difficult because Barry was so close to his dad. "He was my childhood hero and a very positive influence in my life."

Friends urged Barry to move to a different house to make a new start in life, but he resisted their suggestions because "a house is just bricks and mortar." His logical engineering mindset had little space for emotional things like the mood a house could create. But eventually, he did make the move and made a commitment to meet new people. When he was invited to a party in his new neighborhood, he agreed to go, even though, by nature, he's a shy introvert. At that party, he got into a lengthy conversation with a Christian woman who asked him what he thought about Jesus. "She was straight to the point, but for some reason that didn't seem awkward. So, I responded by being very forthcoming with my atheism." Barry coolly repeated Dawkins's arguments to this woman, but as he heard them come out of his own mouth, he found them less than persuasive—to himself! "I wasn't satisfied with the answers I was giving her, so I figured I just needed to go back home and do more study." He figured he was just rusty in making these arguments. Barry concluded he needed to read more

Dawkins. So he did. Quite a bit. He also watched video debates between Dawkins and the Oxford mathematician and Christian John Lennox. The more he watched, the less solid his atheism felt.

Then, at Christmastime, the bold Christian woman from the party sent Barry a Christmas present of two books, C. S. Lewis's *Mere Christianity* and a short paperback simply titled *Life*. He did not know the latter was a book from the Bible, the Gospel of John. In fact, even after reading it, he didn't know it was from the Bible. Such was his level of ignorance of the Christian faith. "I was convinced in my atheism, and I didn't see any harm in reading the things she gave me. I was going to pull it all apart because I was so confident in my own intellect and of the incorrectness of faith."

Dismantling Lewis's logic in *Mere Christianity* wasn't as easy as he had expected.

> I read the book for the purpose of finding the holes, but I couldn't find any. What really got me was that Christianity, the way Lewis presented it, wasn't as silly as Dawkins made it out to be. There was a coherence to it. I still wasn't a believer, but I now gave Christianity a respect that I would have dismissed earlier. I had arrogantly thought intellectuals weren't Christians and didn't believe in God. But there were intellectuals out there who were Christians, and it gave me a wake-up call.

Over the next several months, Barry set out to make a personal investigation of the faith. This included a lot of reading[4] and sneaking into the back of a church.

4   Among the most important books he read were John Lennox, *God's Undertaker: Has Science Buried God?* (Oxford: Lion, 2009) and Alister McGrath and Joanna Collicutt

I figured if I was going to learn about Christians, I should hear directly from them. I arrived late and left early. I wanted to remain anonymous. Besides, I was just there to observe. After the first service, a Christmas carol service, I thought, *I'm never coming back here.*

But at that service they announced the start of an eight-week class for people who were "curious about Christianity." Barry had to admit that described him perfectly. So he started attending and was surprised to learn how much evidence there was to support Christian beliefs. "I was oblivious to the historic nature of the faith." He heard about manuscripts, historical evidence for things recorded in the New Testament, extrabiblical evidence for the life of Jesus and many more things. "The scales were tipping," he told me as he watched video debates between Dawkins and Lennox. He felt like Dawkins was losing the debates. "Dawkins sounded desperate, like he *had* to win. But John Lenox sounded confident and at peace, like he knew the truth was on his side whether his opponent believed him or not."

During one of the sessions of the course about Christianity, Barry heard someone speak about prayer. The speaker found himself locked out of his house and his key wouldn't open the lock. So he prayed that God would make the key work. Sure enough, on the second try, the key opened the lock. Barry dismissed this immediately as utter foolishness. "Locks are dodgy things and sometimes keys don't work. This isn't any kind of evidence for God or anything supernatural."

McGrath, *The Dawkins Delusion: Atheist Fundamentalism and the Denial of the Divine* (Downers Grove, IL: InterVarsity Press, 2007).

He told me all this through a Zoom conversation with little emotion. Then he paused. He seemed hesitant to tell me the next part of his story.

> I came back from a run and was covered in sweat and mud, and I got into the shower. I turned on the water and it was ice cold. So, I thought, *Am I supposed to pray about this?* I thought, *God, if you're there, could you fix the water?* But it just continued to run cold.

Again, he hesitated to tell me what happened next.

"I thought, I should say it out loud. And I said something different this time: 'God, I *know* you can do this for me. Please do this for me.'" And then he looked directly into his computer's camera and said, with more emotion than I'd heard up until this point, "That's a strange thing for an atheist to say!" Again he hesitated. "And then the water turned hot. . . . It was weird. It was a real moment for me, but I didn't know what to do with that."

But then his logical engineering mind kicked in, and he reasoned that sometimes hot water heaters take longer to work than at other times. But "it left me open to try again." This time, his attempt to pray had higher stakes. Since his father's death, he grew in deep concern for his mother. She found little strength to handle her grief. Barry called her often to check in, but those calls always felt painful and hopeless. He dreaded making the calls and always needed time after them to recover emotionally. So he prayed and asked God to work in his mother's life and give her something good in her week before his next call.

"Mom, how are you doing?" he began the next call.

"Oh, it's been a very good week. I went out to dinner with your aunt, and then two friends took me out to lunch, and yesterday I joined a gym."

Barry laughed as he got to the word "gym." "My mother joined a gym! That's amazing. And that has lasted until this day." Again he paused. Even through Zoom, I could see his eyes begin to tear up. "The hot water was not life changing, but my mom's life was a massive thing."

Some people have dramatic conversions to Christianity. They stand up at a religious gathering or they pray a prayer and feel a jolt of emotion. Barry's crossing the line from unbelief to belief was remarkably undramatic. He continued to go to the church's worship services and heard teaching about God and sin and Jesus. He was starting to belong there. After a few weeks, someone said to him, "You believe, don't you?" "Good question," Barry replied and, taking a moment, added: "I can't say no to this. Yeah, I do. I believe."

As Barry looks back at that whole chapter in his life—now over a decade later—he sums it up this way: "The defenses of the Christian faith had more explanatory power than Dawkins's atheist arguments."

Here's something I find intriguing. Both Neal's and Barry's stories contain an intertwining of the known and the unknown. More accurately, both have elements with high levels of confidence and some with low levels of confidence. Neal felt quite confident that the Bible has problems in it. But he had to "just accept" that many good things in his life are "mere happenstance." Barry found historical evidence for the Christian faith to be very solid. But he couldn't prove that God was the one who answered his prayers. Both men had some confidence. Neither had absolute certainty.

Doubting Our Doubts

Different belief systems have differing levels of tolerance for doubt. Christianity has had a long track record of adherents with less than absolute certainty. Many have honestly wondered whether they should cling to their faith in the face of difficult circumstances. Even John the Baptist, who boldly, publicly, and controversially proclaimed that Jesus was the Messiah, had doubts. When he was arrested and thrown into prison for his public preaching of an unwelcomed message, he wondered if he'd placed his faith in the right object. He sent word to Jesus asking, "Are you the one who is to come, or should we look for another?"[5]

If you've already heard this story, don't let its familiarity diminish its outrageousness. John was Jesus's cousin. They grew up together. Their childhoods included the fact that both of their births were considered miraculous. Both John's mother and Jesus's mother were convinced that Jesus was the Messiah, the one the Jewish people had expected and longed for across generations. John made statements about Jesus that must have astonished the religious leaders who traveled from Jerusalem to the wilderness to hear this rather unusual preacher. John had the audacity to call them a "brood of vipers" because of their religious hypocrisy.[6]

But then he faltered in his doubts. Jesus responded to John with pointers to his messiahship: "The blind receive their sight and the

5   Matthew 11:3.
6   Matthew 3:7.

lame walk, lepers are cleansed and the deaf hear, and the dead are raised up, and the poor have the good news preached to them."[7]

Did this evidence prove beyond a shadow of doubt that John had no cause to waver? Did it satisfy him? We don't know. He was brutally executed a short time later. But Christians ever since have found ironic comfort amid their doubts when they've pondered, *If even John the Baptist could have some doubts, I too can live with doubts amid faith.*

Another patron saint of doubt was the unnamed man whose son Jesus healed. With words that countless people of faith have uttered ever since, the man said, "I believe; help my unbelief!"[8] If we all need to admit some level of doubt, I suggest that we doubt our doubts. Believers and skeptics should examine their doubts and see just how formative they really are. We may find that they're not as substantive as we have assumed.

Barry's doubt flowed from his assumption that Christianity was only for simpletons who never doubted. He couldn't believe because his doubts were too formative. But when he doubted his doubts and dug deeper to see if Richard Dawkins's views of Christianity were accurate, he found atheism to be flimsier than Christianity.

Thus, we find ourselves at another crucial turn in our journey of questioning faith. We need to admit, however reluctantly,

Amid our doubts, we should seek confidence more than certainty.

For some, this means not settling for merely raising a question. We should seek out the best answers. If some stories in the Bible

7   Matthew 11:5.
8   Mark 9:24.

seem too far-fetched to accept, we should consider that we're not the first ones to have this impression. We should see what the best scholars have to say.

Pointers, Not Proofs

Here's another way to look at this key turn in a journey of belief. If confidence is a more realistic expectation than certainty, perhaps we should look for pointers instead of proofs. A short search on the Internet for debates between atheists and Christians can lead to exchanges about proofs for God's existence. Introductory philosophy textbooks recount so-called proofs by Anselm, Aquinas, Augustine, and others (even some whose names don't begin with *A*). They attach labels like *ontological*, *cosmological*, *moral*, and *teleological*. I've invited friends to such events and even sponsored some. I've been embarrassed when these "proofs" failed to prove. If a skeptic can find one hole in one of the arguments, I've doubted if even Anselm, Aquinas, or Augustine could have turned the tide.

But what if we don't really need a proof? What if we only need pointers that suggest a belief in the supernatural makes more sense than a rejection of the supernatural? What if you can't prove Jesus really said the things the New Testament claims he said, but the archaeological, historical, and manuscript evidence points far more in the direction of acceptance than dismissal? What if you can't prove God created the world with a sense of order or design, but all the complexity and beauty in the physical universe suggest this is more likely than the conclusion that all this happened through chaos and chance?

These are the kinds of arguments Timothy Keller has made in his bestselling books *The Reason for God* and *Making Sense of God*. In a *Wall Street Journal* interview about his Christian faith, he said,

"You can't prove it, but you can reason for it."[9] A public conversation between Keller and Greg Epstein, the humanist chaplain at Harvard, focuses on questions of meaning in life. Specifically, they landed on two summarizing questions: First, "Is there ultimate meaning in life?" and, second, "Can individual people find meaning in life?" Keller, the Christian, answered yes to both questions. Epstein, the humanist, answered no to the first but yes to the second. No, there's no ultimate meaning in life, but, yes, individual people *can* find meaning. He clarified that individual people create their own meaning in life. They don't need a god to provide it.

The exchange between these two men was more than polite. The tone was exemplary and a welcome contrast to the shrill anger usually found on social media. The two friends went out of their way to express respect for one another's ideas. They clearly disagreed, but they did so agreeably. Keller countered Epstein's two answers (No, there is no ultimate meaning, but, yes, people can create their own individual meaning) with something like this: "I acknowledge that this is possible. But in my experiences with people who try to live like this, it becomes an ever increasing no and an ever decreasing yes."[10]

Coherence as a Confidence Booster

If we're seeking confidence more than certainty, one factor can help toward our goal: *coherence*. If all belief systems contain things

---

9 Emily Bobrow, "Pastor Timothy Keller Speaks to the Head and the Heart," *Wall Street Journal*, September 2, 2022, https://www.wsj.com/articles/pastor-timothy-keller-speaks-to-the-head-and-the-heart-11662136046.

10 Admittedly, I am relying on my memory of this event. I cannot find any audio or video recording or transcript of the event. But having read a lot of Keller, I believe my statement accurately reflects his beliefs.

we know and things we can't, we should look to see which systems hold together best or which beliefs resonate with the reality we see all around us. Here is what I mean.

Let's say you're walking in the woods and come upon a turtle sitting atop a tree stump three feet off the ground. Picture it. Knowing what you know about trees and turtles, a few conclusions seem more likely than others. We know trees don't stop growing with a flat surface on top. We know people often cut down trees with saws that make for a flat surface on a tree trunk. We also know that turtles crawl horizontally and can't ascend three-foot vertical planes. We could conclude that (a) someone cut down this tree, and (b) someone lifted the turtle and put it on top of the stump. Or we could conclude that (a) the tree stopped growing and part of it fell off, leaving a flat surface on the stump, and (b) the turtle climbed up the vertical surface until it got to the horizontal plane and stopped for a rest. One conclusion coheres better with what we know about the reality of trees and turtles.

Now let's consider some more important issues than how a turtle got on top of a tree stump. We live in a world with many competing perspectives—some religious and some naturalistic. A Christian perspective says we live in an ordered world created by a good God who made people in his image. The naturalistic perspective believes we evolved by random chance in a universe without any purposeful cause.

We also live in a world where people value equality and respect. Which belief system supports our commonly held values? How did we arrive at believing we should treat people with impartiality and kindness?

We can't know with absolute certainty how or when our world was created or grasp all the complexities of human existence. But I want to suggest that we can have a high level of confidence that it makes more sense to believe we live in a created world with a personal God than to believe we are nothing more than cosmic accidents. I say this because we treat people with dignity and fairness, or at least we believe we should. And values like equality and respect cohere better with the Christian view than the naturalistic one.

Consider how adherents of these two disparate views expound their views. Yuval Noah Harari, a lecturer in history at the Hebrew University of Jerusalem, clearly articulates a naturalistic perspective in his bestselling book *Sapiens: A Brief History of Humankind*. He says:

> According to the science of biology, people were not "created." They have evolved. And they certainly did not evolve to be "equal." The idea of equality is inextricably intertwined with the idea of creation. The Americans got the idea of equality from Christianity, which argues that every person has a divinely created soul, and that all souls are equal before God. However, if we do not believe in the Christian myths about God, creation and souls, what does it mean that all people are "equal"? . . . Similarly, there are no such things as rights in biology. . . . Homo sapiens has no natural rights, just as spiders, hyenas and chimpanzees have no natural rights. But don't tell that to our servants, lest they murder us at night.[11]

11 Yuval Noah Harari, *Sapiens: A Brief History of Humankind* (New York: Harper Perennial, 2015), 109, 111.

By contrast, Glen Scrivener, an Anglican minister and author, writes in his bestselling book *The Air We Breathe: How We All Came to Believe in Freedom, Kindness, Progress, and Equality*:

> Without a God story (and without a very particular God story), humans remain adrift in the world, fending for themselves and valued for their properties only—some valued more and some much less. But if there is . . . someone of supreme value, and if this source of value shares a vital connection to humanity, then another possibility is opened up. By association with God, we can see humans as worth far more than the flesh-and-blood material of each of us, and far more than our blood-and-sweat toil.[12]

Questioning Certainty

Scrivener makes arguments that the Christian religion—and not naturalism—is historically and logically the basis for values of compassion, consent, enlightenment, science, freedom, and progress. Oddly, Harari agrees with Scrivener—up to a point. They both say that without God, belief in human rights has no basis. The question is, which view coheres with the world in which we live?

What do you think? Do you agree that all viewpoints contain some unprovable assumptions? If so, can you identify some of those assumptions in your own beliefs? Are you willing to doubt your doubts? Can you accept a level of confident belief without requiring absolute certainty? Ponder these questions as we move ahead to comparing different religious perspectives.

12 Glen Scrivener, *The Air We Breathe: How We All Came to Believe in Freedom, Kindness, Progress, and Equality* (n.p.: Good Book, 2022), 50–51.

4

The Question of Differences

*What If Our Similarities Aren't
as Helpful as We Think?*

THE STORY OF THE BLIND MEN and the elephant had always captured Bill's imagination. He loved it when his pastor wove the story into her sermons. She told it so often as an expression of her attitude about religion that she could simply allude to it and her congregation would nod along agreeably.

The story probably has its origins in Hinduism, but I've heard Christians, Buddhists, and more than a few rabbis claim it fits well with their traditions. In case you're not familiar with the story, it tells of six blind men coming upon an elephant. They feel their way around the elephant's tusk, tail, side, and ear, and they draw different conclusions about what an elephant is. The blind man holding the tail says, "An elephant is like a snake." The one with the tusk says, "An elephant is like a spear." The one by the side says, "An elephant is like a wall." And so on.

When the story is told, the teller usually brings the narrative to a climax with lessons like these:

No one sees the whole elephant. No one has the full picture. And that's what the different religions of the world are like. Christianity, Judaism, Islam, Buddhism, Hinduism, and all the others only see part of reality; one religion cannot state conclusively what God is like or what life is all about. But if we'd just listen to each other, we could put our partial views together and get a fuller picture.

As you might guess, this parable is a favorite in comparative religions classes. John Godfrey Saxe expressed both the thoughts and sentiments of this story in a poem with these two final stanzas:

And so these men of Indostan
Disputed loud and long,
Each in his own opinion
Exceeding stiff and strong,
Though each was partly in the right,
And all were in the wrong!

So, oft in theologic wars
The disputants, I ween,
Rail on in utter ignorance
Of what each other mean,
And prate about an elephant
Not one of them has seen![1]

---

1 John Godfrey Saxe, "The Blind Men and the Elephant," in *The Best Loved Poems of the American People*, ed. Hazel Felleman (New York: Doubleday, 1936), 521–22.

The final appeal calls for humility and a turn away from the arrogance that individual religions have when they claim the truth.

Bill never tired of hearing this story. Until he heard a different take on it. For part of the year, he and his wife, Jana, lived in a condo on the beautiful beach paradise of Treasure Cay in the Bahamas. Away from their home church, they attended a Christian chapel that invited guest preachers from a variety of Christian denominations to lead Sunday morning worship. Bill and Jana loved the mix of perspectives, from liberal, mainline Protestant to evangelical nondenominational.

One Sunday, the guest preacher told the blind-men-and-the-elephant story but then commented:

> I was drawn to this story when I first heard it. I liked it until someone challenged me on it. They asked me, "How can we tell that story?" I didn't understand their question. They elaborated, "The only way we can tell that story is if *we* claim to see the whole elephant. How else could we know that none of those blind men saw the whole elephant? In other words, we who tell the story are really the *most* arrogant of all. We're guilty of the very sin for which we're judging all those blind men—claiming to know what the whole elephant looks like."

The preacher paused and added:

> I didn't like hearing someone critique one of my favorite stories. But I had to admit they had a valid point. Isn't it a little patronizing to say all those religious men are blind but we, the objective observers telling the story, can see? When we tell

that story, are we saying Jesus was blind? That Muhammad was blind? Or Buddha? Are we claiming to be smarter and more enlightened than those religious leaders?

Bill felt his world crumbling. It was the worst worship service he'd experienced and the most disturbing sermon he'd ever heard. Unlike so many other Sundays, this time, as he walked out of the chapel, he did *not* shake the preacher's hand. But he thought about the sermon for the rest of the day.

The next morning, he knocked on the door of the apartment the church provided for their guest preachers. He asked for a retelling of that part of the sermon about the blind men and the elephant. The preacher invited him in for some coffee and simply restated what he'd shared the day before, adding: "It is rather disturbing to have something you've held dear for a long time dismantled, isn't it? It certainly was for me." Bill nodded and said he needed to think about it more. He acknowledged that if we claim to see the whole elephant, we are in fact guilty of our own kind of religious arrogance.

I know the details of this encounter between the preacher and Bill because I was that guest preacher. I remember Bill's face when we chatted over that cup of coffee. I was impressed that he was willing to question something he'd believed for a long time. I was more impressed because he was in his midsixties, and he'd held this view for decades. He told me this was the last year he and his wife would be coming to Treasure Cay. They'd reached the stage of life when they needed to be close to the best medical attention they could find. This tiny island, while stunningly beautiful, lacked the doctors and hospitals they would need in the years ahead.

"We want to have home field advantage for the fourth quarter," he told me with a smile. I've lost touch with him, but I hope he was able to wrestle with how different religions differ.

Differences Make a Difference

Many people are convinced that the different religions of the world are merely "roads on the same mountain that all lead to the top." In fact, that image is presented with approval in one of the most frequently used textbooks for religious studies courses, *The Religions of Man* by Huston Smith. We're encouraged to find the commonalities of the different religions rather than focus on where they differ.

Respect for one another, a high value for spirituality, pursuing peace in the world, and other "universals" should form the center of everyone's religious life, according to this framework. But the all-roads-up-the-same-mountain analogy suffers from the same weakness as the blind-men-and-the-elephant story. The only way a person can tell that all these roads make their way to the top of the same mountain is if he, somehow, omnisciently hovers over the mountain and sees the zenith where all the roads meet.

As I've talked to people about their individual faith journeys, this all-roads view resonates with very few. It's championed only by those who subscribe to no particular religion at all. Sincere adherents of Judaism, Buddhism, Islam, Christianity, Hinduism, and pretty much every other religion do *not* see themselves on a road up the same mountain as the others. They think they're on the best (and, in some cases, only) road to make it to the top. When they compare their religion with others, they believe they've found the truth and feel bad for people who have not. It seems that the *differences* between religions, not their similarities, are most helpful in propelling people through terrains of doubt.

Jesus and Yoga

For Susan, it was the contrast between Christianity and Yoga that helped her move forward. She grew up in a churchgoing family but never really grasped the core of Christian teaching. In particular, she never understood why Jesus died and what difference that made. It sure was stressed a lot, as she participated in odd rituals and repeated rote prayers. But the many depictions of Jesus hanging on a cross only seemed like graphic displays of cruel injustice from a politically corrupt culture during an unenlightened society long ago.

She told me that when she went off to college, she thought she already knew the Christian message and rejected it. But, she added, "I realize now that I didn't really understand it." Her psychology, sociology, and philosophy courses only convinced her that Christianity was, as Marx put it, "an opiate of the masses" and not something any intelligent person should subscribe to. In a short time, she identified herself as an atheist (although, oddly, she still went to a variety of churches because she liked the cultural aspects, the music, and the social connections).

After earning a PhD in one of the social sciences, she got a tenure-track position at a university in an area of the country she described as "New Age Heaven." "I got really into crystals, the New Age, and Reiki, all these healing modalities, weekend retreats with spiritual people—really deep into that, and I was into this for ten years."

Susan's speech sped up as she described her daily ritual, which included an hour of meditation and thirty minutes of chanting to a variety of gods. But then she paused a bit and said more softly, "But I was getting dissatisfied with Yoga because I was becoming more and more aware of my sin." She told me some things she had done—quite a list—and wondered how she could be set free from the guilt she felt. "All the things I had done were weighing me down, weighing, weighing, weighing." Her voice trailed off, and I wondered if she was about to cry.

Others into Yoga told her to meditate more or chant more. When she asked the pointed question "What is the remedy for sin?" she received blank stares and shrugged shoulders. Yoga had no answers to her most pressing question. Not only that, but she was told that her daily rituals were supposed to give her inner peace and, as she said, "that wasn't happening! And we'd been at this for ten years!"

Somewhere in the midst of that disillusionment, her family moved to a new neighborhood and met new neighbors. At one local gathering, Susan sensed she should introduce herself to a woman she'd never seen before. "I walked up to this total stranger and said: 'I'm sorry. I think I'm supposed to meet you.'" Susan never even considered this might seem odd to this other person. All her years of meditation and chanting opened her up to listen to inner voices or promptings from a spiritual world, so this just seemed normal. Looking back at it, she admitted to me this must have seemed bizarre.

Her new acquaintance didn't flinch. Holly, her newfound friend, was a Christian who told me: "I can't explain it, but I connect to a lot to people who are very spiritual. So meeting Susan just seemed to be another one of those encounters. Actually, it seemed like we were both drawn to each other—like magnets."

Very quickly, they found out they lived on the same street, worked at the same university, and had children around the same age. They started taking walks together and got into very deep conversations. Holly asked her a lot of questions about Yoga and her beliefs, which, in turn, led Susan to ask Holly about her beliefs.

Holly used the word *atonement* several times as she explained her beliefs, but Susan had no idea what that term meant. "She kept using this word *atonement*, and I was like, what does *that* mean?" Holly admitted it's an unusual concept for most people to comprehend. It actually took months of long walks together before Susan started to grasp the meaning of this core tenet of Christianity. "How could I have gone to a Christian church for all those years and never understood this?" she said several times during our conversation. But that wasn't the most important question for her. The thing she needed to understand was what atonement actually meant in someone's everyday experience.

Holly tried coming at it from a number of different angles.

I told her Jesus paid for her sins, but I'm not sure she knew what I meant. I tried talking about a substitute, and she said that her faith had something like that. So I latched on to that and tried to say: "Jesus represents you to God, the Father. But it's as a sacrifice for your sins. He took the punishment you deserved so you don't have to."

Susan still didn't seem to comprehend and asked, "Can we still be friends if you worship Jesus and I follow a different spiritual path?" Holly answered, "Of course." But that seemed to surprise Susan. She was puzzled by acceptance between people who believed such vastly contradictory things. Holly suggested that Susan should try to read some of the Bible, perhaps starting at the Gospel of John. Susan reported back that reading the Bible felt like reading a foreign language. She couldn't make any sense of it at all. After a while, Susan simply added a tiny statue of Jesus to her many other idols in her living room altar. Why not add one more deity, she thought. But another Christian friend told her that wouldn't work. "You have to choose. Jesus made claims about himself that set him apart from all other people, or gods. He claimed to be God, that he's the only way, that he's the only one who atoned for sins." There was that word again—*atone*! Inexplicably, that was a turning point for Susan. Her Bible reading started making sense. She was particularly struck by this statement toward the end of the Gospel of John:

> Jesus did many other signs in the presence of the disciples, which are not written in this book; but these are written so that you may believe that Jesus is the Christ, the Son of God, and that by believing you may have life in his name.[2]

Eventually it started to click. But not without difficulty. Susan said:

> I had been taught, when I went to some churches, that there were certain sins that were beyond the reach of God's forgiveness. They were sins that would send you to hell . . . and I had committed at least one of those sins. And now I'm telling this Christian woman about my sin, and I was sure she was going to reject me.

2 John 20:30–31.

But instead, Holly told her: "That's the whole point of coming to the Lord. He can forgive you." (The teaching that some sins are beyond God's ability to forgive is not what orthodox Christianity teaches.) After a lot of questions and elaborate answers, Susan became a Christian. Here's how she put it into words:

> I was doing all that Yoga stuff for ten years, and I never felt better or found inner peace. But then I spend two minutes with Jesus—I asked for his forgiveness—and after receiving him, it was like a boulder [she was choking back tears] . . . this boulder left me. I couldn't believe it! This guy, Jesus, is real, and all I needed to say was: "Lord, I'm sorry. I need your forgiveness." And it was instant.

As in previous chapters, we've arrived at a vantage point in our questioning of faith. We need to turn around on our upward hike and look back at the terrain we've just come through and notice:

Observing the differences between religions may be more helpful than looking for their similarities.

Susan concluded her story this way:

> Can I convince other people of this? They'll just say, "Well, that was your experience." Well, it was my experience, but it also had substance to it. And that substance was about who Jesus is and what he said about himself. He didn't say he was just a teacher. He said he was the Son of God. I had to decide who was telling the truth. I had been believing what

my yogi told me about Jesus for so long, but I had never read the Bible. Now I saw that the biggest difference between Yoga and Christianity was that Christianity has a provision for sin. Yoga doesn't.

Jesus and Muhammad

For Farid, differences between religions drove his journey—from atheism to Islam and then from Islam to Christianity. Raised in a nominally Muslim home in Russia where atheism was the default belief system, Farid viewed Islam as backward and superstitious. In his early teens, he wondered about death and found atheism's complete denial of any life after the grave to be unsatisfying. Influenced by Russian writers like Dostoyevsky, he wondered why we think so much about death. The vast chasm between atheism's nothingness after death and Islam's hope for heaven prompted years of intense study. He found atheism to be too simplistic to explain life's complexities.

When Farid entered the university, a friend asked him, rather pointedly, if he practiced what he said he believed. In response, Farid began to practice Islam more and more, finding genuine joy from seeking after God's will. By the time he transferred to a university in America, he identified openly as a Muslim. On campus, he joined the Muslim Student Association (MSA), began praying five times a day, and faithfully read the Qur'an. "I was excited about all the things I heard. I finally not only claimed to be a Muslim but also practiced my faith in my daily life."[3]

3   All of Farid's quotes are from "How I Came to Believe That Jesus Really Did Die on the Cross and Why It Matters," Answering Islam, https://www.answering-islam.org. I also verified these statements in personal conversations with him.

It did not take long for Farid, with his growing zeal, to become a Muslim evangelist. "Sharing Islam with others had become one of my top priorities." Farid showed it, too, by participating in MSA-sponsored events and eagerly sharing his faith in many personal conversations, with just about anyone. Farid particularly liked engaging with Christians.

> I was obviously convinced that they were wrong because they did not believe Muhammad was the prophet. Worst of all, they believed Jesus was the Son of God. All Christians were committing "shirk," the worst and most unforgivable sin—and I desired for them to come to know the truth.

Wanting to know how best to convert Christians to Islam drove Farid to intense study of his faith. He listened to recordings and read books by a leading Muslim scholar, Ahmed Deedat, and others who had widespread success in promoting Islam. He grew in confidence in answering Christians' questions and pointing out flaws in their beliefs.

> I had lists of apparent contradictions in the Bible, proofs of forgery, history of persecution by Christians in medieval times, and the list went on and on. I felt confident Christians were wrong. However, there was one question Christians asked that I didn't have enough information to answer. It was the question about the death and resurrection of Jesus.

According to Islam, Jesus did not die on the cross. It only appeared so. Islam teaches that Christians have been deceived and confused about this ever since.

So Farid decided to investigate Christianity with the analytical intensity that helped him understand Islam so well. He found that the death and resurrection of Jesus were no minor issues, as he'd been taught through Islam. The more he read and talked to Christians, the more he found these two events to be the very core and center of Christian belief. At the same time, he was warned by his Muslim friends and leaders not to study this issue any further. These weren't just personal warnings issued against Farid. All Muslims, he learned, were discouraged from investigating the significance of Jesus's death and resurrection. "Effectively it looked as if Islam was denying the central point of Christianity without addressing it."

Farid spent over two years trying to find satisfying responses to Islam's claims about Christianity, especially the claim that the earliest Christians didn't believe in Jesus's resurrection. Muslims believe that the resurrection "lie" came along later. But Farid's investigations could not find evidence of a single Christian sect who did not believe that Jesus Christ died on a cross and rose from the dead, or who believed "anything close to what I thought the 'original' Christians would've believed according to Islam." Further study of the Old Testament's prophecies of a coming Messiah's sacrificial death only raised more disturbing doubts.

Most of Farid's friends didn't think his questions were important. Their superficial and poorly argued answers brought him little satisfaction. "I did not like my doubts," Farid told me. "I asked God to take my doubts away and make things clear." But Farid's searching took him in the opposite direction, into less clarity and more doubt. "After two and a half years of thinking and searching, the evidence I found for Christianity was too weighty to be discounted." Farid could no longer be a Muslim but couldn't claim any religion. "I became an agnostic who believed that God existed, that a true faith existed, but I just didn't know which faith was right. I spent the next year and a half asking God to reveal to me which faith I should follow. It was painful."

Farid's journey out of this pain began intellectually. He concluded the Christian doctrines are true and that the Muslim ones distort the truth. He found compelling and substantive reasons to accept that Jesus is indeed the unique and only Son of God, that his death and resurrection really happened, that Old Testament prophecies find their fulfillment in Jesus, and that the New Testament presents accurate history. More pointedly, he knew he needed forgiveness for sin and that Jesus's death provided that forgiveness.

The next stage in Farid's journey is harder to categorize. "I asked God to rescue me if he wanted to, because I couldn't do it on my own strength. I'd been using my intellect to jump over walls and go through doors, but none of my efforts succeeded." In this attitude of surrender, Farid sensed what he could only describe as God's love for him.

Today, many claim that Christians and Muslims worship the same God. It's another version of the all-religions-are-the-same argument. Some merely hope this conviction will defuse some of the hostility in our powder-keg world. But, as Farid discovered, when we investigate the two faiths, we discover that they disagree on essential points, not the least of which is the very character of God. Christians believe God is loving. The most frequently quoted verse from the New Testament is John 3:16. The verse puts God's love front and center of Christian doctrine:

"For God so loved the world, that he gave his only Son, that whoever believes in him should not perish but have eternal life." The New Testament goes even further in 1 John 4:8, claiming "God is love." It's not just that God acts in loving ways; in his very essence, he is love.

Does Islam make any such claim about Allah? It may not be popular to admit, but the facts point us toward a negative answer. Andy Bannister, an Islamic studies scholar, writes, "[Love] is an attribute of God identified by the Bible hundreds of times."

> [But] unlike the Bible, the Qur'an is very reticent about talking of Allah and love. In fact, the main Arabic word for love, *ahabba*, is used with Allah as the subject of the verb just forty-two times and, of those occurrences, twenty-three are negative, describing the kind of people Allah does *not* love [unbelievers and prodigals].

The other nineteen occurrences are conditional, describing the behavior—doing good deeds and fighting for Allah's way in the world—that is required to earn Allah's love. Bannister concludes, "The Qur'an simply has no conception of Allah offering anything remotely like an unconditional love to humanity."[4]

When Farid became a Christian, his intellectual conclusions were woven together with joy. But since then, he's been met with disappointment, disapproval, and bewilderment from his family and other Muslims. This continues to this day, decades after his conversion. His conversion has been a sacrifice, but he says:

4   Andy Bannister, *Do Muslims and Christians Worship the Same God?* (London: SPCK, 2021), 62–63.

I have also experienced kindness, gentleness, and deep sincere love. . . . God is no longer a remote creator who closely watches my life, weighing my bad deeds against my good deeds. He is an infinite being who cares about me personally, and who wants me to be fully committed to him.

Jesus and Judaism

I attended Hebrew school three afternoons per week for five years in anticipation of my bar mitzvah at age thirteen. There I learned to participate in synagogue worship and read the Scriptures in Hebrew. I was prepared for a lifetime of Jewish liturgy and culture, and I sought to connect with God through our traditions and rituals.

But no matter how hard I tried to obey the commandments, God always seemed distant and alien. Connecting with the Almighty seemed vague at best. When I was sixteen, I decided to give Yom Kippur, the holiest day of the Jewish year, one more shot. I attempted complete adherence to all that day's commandments—and there were a lot of them. On Yom Kippur, you fasted, didn't ride in a car, stayed in synagogue for most of the day (plus the evening before), and repented of all the sins you could recall from the past year.

When I walked home at the end of the holiday, I felt that all my religious observances didn't work. God seemed no closer than he'd been twenty-four hours before. What did I do wrong? What sin didn't I confess? What prayer didn't I chant? Then, I looked down at my shoes.

Though the command doesn't appear in the Bible, rabbinic tradition taught that on Yom Kippur, you were not to wear leather shoes. Some rabbis said leather shoes were too much of a luxury, that they were unsuited for the humility Yom Kippur required. As I was walked home dejected that day, I thought: *This is the stupidest thing in the world! You've got to be kidding me. Is that how you connect with God: Remember this rule? Don't do these things? Wear the right shoes? There must be some other way.*

A short time later, a Christian friend invited me to his church's youth group. He assured me that the activities weren't religious and that the girls were cute. So I went. He was right about both the activities and the girls. But the gatherings weren't totally de-void of religion, because these people—both the youth and their parents—talked about God a lot. They claimed to have a personal relationship with God, and they seemed to live like it was true. They prayed about everything, and they prayed in English! I found it all appealing, and I began to ask questions about how they could have such a personal connection with God. Their answers always centered on Jesus. They returned again and again to that moment in history when Jesus died on a cross. They said this fulfilled Old Testament prophecy and satisfied God's righteousness in ways no person, other than the Messiah, could.

I told them I didn't believe in Jesus because I was Jewish. This line of reasoning had worked with other Christians who tried to convert me. But this group politely and confidently responded with questions like "So?" They would go on to tell me that Jesus was Jewish, and so were his disciples. In fact, they claimed that most people who believed Jesus was the Messiah in the first three centuries were Jewish. These Christians challenged me to read the New Testament, and they gave me a copy. I politely accepted their gift but knew I'd never open it. My rabbi warned me that the New Testament was the source of much antisemitism, and I believed him.

So my journey of faith took a years-long hiatus—until midway through my college experience. Faith stories move at varying speeds, and mine slowed almost to a crawl. But the difference between a religion centered on what I needed to do (Judaism) and one centered on what someone else did for me (Jesus's dying on a cross) rubbed like a pebble in my shoe that couldn't be ignored.

Different Paths, Different Mountains

Stephen Prothero, seasoned professor of religion at Boston University, has written responding to the commonly held view that all religions are the same: "This is a lovely sentiment but it is dangerous, disrespectful, and untrue."[5] He points out that the eight major world religions don't come close to agreeing on core issues like God's nature, the basic problems religion seeks to solve, and how to relate to God. For some religions, relating to God isn't even a meaningful category.

Judaism insists that there is only one God, and worship of other gods is one of the worst sins. This God is a personal God with a name, Yahweh. "Many Buddhists believe in no god, and many Hindus believe in thousands."[6] With just a small amount of study, you'll find that the Christian's goal of *salvation* is substantively different from the Buddhist's aim at *enlightenment*, or the Muslim's goal of *submission*, or numerous other religions' pursuits of *self-discovery*, *self-mastery*, or *self-actualization*. In fact, according

---

5   Stephen Prothero, *God Is Not One: The Eight Rival Religions That Run the World and Why Their Differences Matter* (New York: HarperCollins, 2010), 2–3.

6   Prothero, *God Is Not One*, 2.

to Judaism and Christianity, looking inward to the self is looking in the wrong direction.

Prothero concludes, "If practitioners of the world's religions are all mountain climbers, then they are on very different mountains, climbing very different peaks, and using very different tools and techniques in their ascents."[7] Pointedly, he writes, "One of the most common misconceptions about the world's religions is that they plumb the same depths, ask the same questions. They do not."[8]

Seeing the Whole Elephant

Here's what I wish I'd said to Bill over that cup of coffee as he wrestled with the story of the blind men and the elephant: God sees the whole elephant! And he's told us what it looks like. To be sure, God hasn't told us everything there is to know about who he is or what the answers to all of life's mysteries are. The Bible itself says that there are things God hasn't revealed anywhere.[9] But the God who has revealed himself through the Bible is not a God who hides. He eagerly makes himself known so people can know him and enjoy a personal relationship with him. He has told us *enough* about the "elephant" that we don't have to feel like blind men groping in the dark.

Questioning Assumptions

Questioning faith takes boldness to examine long-held assumptions. Have you believed that all religions are basically the same? If so, on what basis have you drawn that conclusion? Has this

---

7   Prothero, *God Is Not One*, 12.

8   Prothero, *God Is Not One*, 24.

9   Deuteronomy 29:29.

chapter prompted you to revisit your beliefs? Are there other assumptions you've made that might need closer scrutiny?

As we turn the next corner in our exploration of faith, we will consider which religious perspective best handles the difficult realities of pain and suffering; this is a place where the differences between religions make a big difference. The elevation on this next leg of our hike takes a significantly steep ascent. Pause to catch your breath, but please don't stop. Though the topic may be unpleasant, it shouldn't be ignored.

5

The Question of Pain

What If We Need More Than Reasons?

"ANY BELIEF I HAD IN GOD died with my uncle." Aleena shared these words with a blank stare. "I loved my uncle," she added. "He was so kind to me, and he always made me smile. But then he got cancer, and watching his body get so weak was horrible." Now Aleena's voice got softer, she spoke more slowly, and I felt her grief. "My uncle was a devout Muslim. Our whole family is Muslim. But I can't believe in Allah or any god that would allow someone to die the way my uncle did." Aleena sounded more angry than sad. Then, rather suddenly, her tone switched and she stated matter-of-factly, "So that's how I became an atheist, and that's why I started the Atheists' Society here at the college."

Aleena and I met to plan a debate on campus. It was cosponsored by a Christian organization I represented and Aleena's newly formed Atheists' Society. She wanted to keep our conversation focused on logistics—where the event would be held, how long it would last, and how we might publicize it. I wanted to explore her beliefs, so I asked her if atheism had helped her with her grief. My question seemed to surprise her. "What do you mean?" she asked. "I hope I'm not being insensitive," I replied. "And if you'd rather not talk about it, I'd be fine if we stuck to planning the event. But I can tell you're still upset about your uncle's death. It must have been horrible to watch his health deteriorate. I'm sorry you had to go through that."

"Thank you," she said quickly. "But what did you mean when you asked how atheism has helped me?"

"Well, it sounds like your family's religion didn't bring you any comfort. Is that right?"

"Yes."

"So, I'm wondering if atheism helps you with your grief more than Islam did."

Long pause. "Not really."

"I realize this is a difficult thing to talk about. I wrestle with it a lot. I come from a Jewish background, and the whole history of the Holocaust feels very painful to think about. But I keep struggling so I can find some peace or comfort amid the pain. I'm wondering if atheism has any answers or explanations for why your uncle suffered the way he did."

She nodded that she understood my question. I could tell she was trying to find the right words. "Well, [expletive] happens." Now it was my turn to nod, and I did, hoping that would tell her I understood. "Does '[expletive] happens' help you handle your grief?" I asked.

"Not really," she replied again, this time more slowly and softly than before.

A Problem for Everyone

Over the many years I've listened to people share their struggles and questions about faith, the problem of pain is the objection most frequently raised. That makes a lot of sense. It's a disturbing and ever-present problem. Sooner or later, regardless of how much we may try to avoid thinking about it, everyone will die. As a young child, I learned about the Holocaust—the systematic murder of six million of my people, two-thirds of the population of European Jews. While attending religious instruction at our local synagogue, I watched films of the concentration camps at Auschwitz, Dachau, and the rest. I've personally struggled ever since with the question of why a good God allows so much suffering.

Often the problem of pain is raised as an accusation against people of faith. "How can *you* believe in God in a world with so much evil and suffering?" The implication seems to be that Christians, Jews, Muslims, and adherents of other religions have an insurmountable incongruity between reverent faith and un-avoidable pain. But pain is also a problem for atheists, agnostics, "nones" (see p. 4), and "dones"—those who once identified with a religion but now feel as if they're "finished with that." We all will (or should) attend funerals of people we care about, and, most pointedly, one day people will attend ours.

For several decades, I've had a delightful friendship with a philosophy professor who abandoned his family's Christian faith in his early teens. He and I kick around issues of belief and nonbelief. I ask him questions about his atheism. He challenges my Christian convictions. We once attended a debate about the problem of evil that featured speakers from a variety of perspectives—Christian, Buddhist, atheist, and agnostic. Afterward, I asked him what he thought of the evening, and he simply said, "I don't think the Christian had a good explanation for the problem of evil." I knew I couldn't do any better than the brilliant speaker we'd just heard, so I asked him about the atheist explanation for the problem of evil. He hesitantly admitted, "Atheism doesn't have a good answer either." What followed was a respectful comparison of our two incomplete answers.

A Limited Number of Options

When addressing pain, suffering, and death, most people fall into one of five categories. Each approach is incomplete. No one of them, including the one I hold most tightly, totally satisfies me. But I do find that some are better than others and one is best of all. You might expect my five categories to be religious ones[1]—the Christian view, the Jewish view, the Buddhist view, and so on— but I find a great deal of diversity even within those categories. Two people in the same religious tradition may hold dramatically divergent views about pain. And people's experiences don't often fit neatly with their creedal statements. I've heard Christians articulate views of suffering that fit more closely to a Buddhist perspective. I've met Jewish people whose views come from secular psychology, not the Old Testament or rabbinic writings. I've also been told that there's no one agreed-upon perspective on suffering within religious traditions like Buddhism, Hinduism, and Judaism. So here I offer five perspectives with more generic labels.[2]

1 A very helpful resource on this topic is Peter Kreeft, *Making Sense Out of Suffering* (Cincinnati, OH: Servant, 1986).

2 I am indebted to Tim Keller's approach to this topic in his very helpful book *Walking with God through Pain and Suffering* (New York: Dutton, 2013). My categories do not align exactly with Keller's, and I have assigned different labels.

The moralistic view. Suffering comes as a consequence of some-one's actions. It's caused by people, and therefore it could have been avoided. This is a common view, and perhaps the oldest one. It's the perspective offered by Job's friends. Job must have com-mitted some sin, they tell him, and that's why his children died, his property was destroyed, and his body is afflicted with disease.[3] In the Hindu tradition, current suffering may even be the result of (Karma for) a person's actions in a previous life.

The reframing view. We must think about suffering and pain differently. When we do, this will alleviate our pain. The reframing view takes many forms, from very religious to completely secular. M. Scott Peck articulated a Buddhist version of the reframing perspective at the beginning of his bestselling book *The Road Less Traveled*:

Life is difficult.

This is a great truth, one of the greatest truths. It is a great truth because once we truly see this truth, we transcend it. Once we truly know that life is difficult—once we truly understand and accept it—then life is no longer difficult.[4]

Not everyone who holds the reframing view identifies as a Buddhist. It finds its way into the thinking of many who claim no

---

3   For example, one friend, Eliphaz, summarized the whole issue of suffering with these words: "Those who plow iniquity / and sow trouble reap the same" (Job 4:8).

4   M. Scott Peck, *The Road Less Traveled: A New Psychology of Love, Traditional Values and Spiritual Growth*, 25th anniversary ed. (New York: Touchstone, 2003), 15. In a footnote, Peck adds, "The first of the 'Four Noble Truths' which Buddha taught was 'Life is suffering.'"

particular religious affiliation. For example, in the movie *Collateral Beauty*, a character who embodies the reality of death tells the main character, Howard, a grieving father who lost his young daughter to cancer, "Nothing's ever really dead if you look at it right."[5]

The healing view. We don't know why there is so much suffering in the world (and it may not matter), but we can work to alleviate it. This view spends little energy on philosophical or theological discussions about why the world is broken. Advocates for the healing view want to spend their energies fixing what is broken. Many Jewish people pursue such efforts under the banner of "Tikkun Olam," a Hebrew expression that can be translated "to heal the world." People from many faith traditions (or none) seek to minimize suffering in the world through medical practice and research, relief efforts during emergencies, offering help to those in poverty, legal efforts to fight injustices like sex trafficking, and many other world-improving works.

The secular view. The reality of evil and suffering is one of the strongest arguments (if not *the* strongest argument) against a belief in God. Richard Dawkins clearly expresses the harsh evolutionary perspective on pain and suffering this way: "In a universe of blind forces and genetic replication, some people are going to get hurt, other people are going to get lucky, and you won't find any rhyme or reason in it, nor any justice."[6]

---

5   *Collateral Beauty*, written by Allan Loeb, directed by David Frankel, produced by Bard Dorros et al. (New Line Cinema, 2016).

6   Richard Dawkins, *River Out of Eden: A Darwinian View of Life* (New York: Basic Books, 1995), 132–33.

The redemptive view. The world is not as it's supposed to be, and suffering is an outrage. But suffering can also be redemptive. It points to an afterlife, when pain and suffering will finally be defeated. This view is found in the Old and New Testaments, and it serves as part of the foundation of Judaism and Christianity. The Hebrew Scriptures teach that a personal God created the world and pronounced all his creation (including people) "good." He gave people the dignity of choice to obey his commands or reject them. The first people (and all people since then) chose, to some degree, disobedience and rebellion against God. And the world has been out of whack ever since. But the Bible also teaches that God has begun a work of redemption that can extend to individual people for all eternity. While this life may include great suffering, an eternal afterlife, free from pain, is offered for those who trust in God's plan of salvation.

An Argument from Outliers

Before we evaluate these five views, we must remember that we're talking about real and painful experiences people face. Some do so as a matter of existence, facing pain through each moment of every day of their entire lives. We must dig into theories about suffering and pain, but we can't leave the discussion there. We also need to find ways that help us answer more than the why question: *Why would a good God allow evil and suffering?* We also need answers for the how questions: *How can someone get through trials and suffering? How do we handle pain, disease, and death? How should we respond when we come face-to-face with evil?* In our journey of questioning faith, here's another milestone:

To face suffering and pain, we need both perspective and power—perspective to make sense of the suffering, and power to handle it.

I've had the privilege of meeting and befriending people who somehow hold on to their strong faith even amid disease, pain, suffering, and loss. It's important for us to listen to their stories of perseverance in belief despite suffering. I have a close friend who has battled the painful realities of cerebral palsy since his birth over forty years ago. He lives with significant physical limitations, frequent discomfort, and the ever-present reminder that his story will get much worse before his life comes to an end. Yet, this man is one of the most joyful people I know. It's not a trite happiness due to distraction. He has a profound joy in the midst of pain. When I've asked him what keeps him holding on to his Christian faith, he's responded with a quote from one of the Gospels. After Jesus fed five thousand people, he preached one of his most difficult and demanding sermons. As a result, some packed up and left. It's one thing to come to Jesus for free food. It's another to devote your life to following him. In that moment, Jesus posed a question to his closest friends: "Do you want to go away as well?" Peter, often the first to speak, replied: "Lord, to whom shall we go? You have the words of eternal life."[7]

My friend returns to this statement often. It glues him to God in transformative ways. In a recent conversation, he told me: "The alternatives just aren't as good. I could get angry at God and shake my fist at him for giving me this disease. But that wouldn't make

7   John 6:67–68.

things any better for me, would it?" Instead, my friend finds great strength from close connection to God through prayer, studying the Bible, gathering with his church for times of worship, and looking for God's fingerprints in all of life.

I could quote many others who face pain and suffering, injustice, cruelty, or evil of the vilest kind, but who nevertheless cling to God and find his presence to be a source of strength and hope.[8] Another friend has battled multiple sclerosis for over three decades. Before doctors could identify her problem as MS, she needed to have an MRI. Feeling anxious about getting an MRI, she wondered, *What will the doctors find?* She recalled, "As I went into that MRI tube, I prayed, God, I'm glad you're not a stranger to me." Stories of physical pain share dynamics with the stories of those who face the harsh realities of evil and injustice. One of the remarkable themes in American history is the widespread reception of Christianity by African American slaves who freely embraced the faith held by slaveholders.[9] Why someone like Frederick Douglass would embrace Christianity, the so-called "faith of the slaveowner who whipped him every day except Sunday (because it was the Sabbath),"[10] is a question that must be addressed and answered. Douglass found ways to distinguish truth from hypocrisy.

---

8   Consider the remarkable story of Joni Eareckson Tada, who found God more than fifty years ago after a diving accident that left her as a quadriplegic. Her book *Joni: An Unforgettable Story* (Grand Rapids, MI: Zondervan, 2021), originally published in 1976, is a bestseller for good reason, and her other writing should not be ignored.

9   The Bible does not support chattel slavery as it was practiced in the southern US before the Civil War. See Gavin Ortlund, "Why It's Wrong to Say the Bible Is Pro-Slavery," TGC, June 7, 2018, https://www.thegospelcoalition.org/article/why-wrong-say-bible -pro-slavery/.

10   David W. Blight, *Frederick Douglass: Prophet of Freedom* (New York: Simon & Schuster, 2018), 65.

Encountering a black lay preacher, Charles Johnson, who spoke with him in "tones of holy affection," Douglass "underwent what he called a conversion to 'faith in Jesus Christ, as the Redeemer, Friend, and Savior of those who diligently seek him."[11] Douglass could have chosen bitterness, but instead he was able to reflect on his life in his later years, "My joys have far exceeded my sorrows and my friends have brought me far more than my enemies have taken from me."[12]

Weighing the Options

Having considered the reality that people who face suffering need both perspective and power, let's evaluate the five views of suffering, looking for answers to both the *why* and the *how* questions.

The moralistic view. First, it should be acknowledged that *some* suffering certainly does come to people because of foolish choices they make. Some suffering is indeed "their own fault." If you decide to drink a lot of alcohol and then drive a car, you may get into an accident, get hurt, or hurt someone else. When we experience pain and suffering, it's worth asking if there is something we could have done differently to avoid the mess we're in.

But if we *always* apply this perspective to *every* form of suffering, we've offered an overly simplistic answer to a multifaceted, complex problem. The moralistic view fails to address disasters like tsunamis and hurricanes. It fails to account for the seemingly random ways some people suffer, and others don't. Some people are healed and others die of the same disease, though they've fol-

11 Blight, *Frederick Douglass*, 53.
12 Blight, *Frederick Douglass*, 610.

lowed the same course of treatment, offered prayers to the same God, thought the same positive thoughts, or channeled the same sources of cosmic energy. When suffering people are told it's their own fault, this can pile guilt on already difficult circumstances. Such insensitivity can also trigger anger that drains them of energy they need to spend in other, more helpful ways. The moralistic view falls terribly short of providing meaningful perspective or helpful power to handle suffering.

The reframing view. How we think about suffering can make a tremendous difference in how we handle it and, ideally, overcome it. We need to carefully examine our default modes of thinking and change some unhealthy or unproductive internal messages that may dominate our minds. We can learn some helpful techniques from those who promote mindfulness.

But a change in thinking can only go so far. Some suffering is bad no matter how we perceive it. In fact, some efforts to change our thinking can lead to harmful denials of reality. M. Scott Peck's endorsement of the fact that "life is difficult" is helpful. Going further to insist that "once we truly know that life is difficult . . . then life is no longer difficult" is naive. In *Collateral Beauty*, Howard rejects the claim that "nothing's ever really dead if you look at it right." In a memorable tirade, he argues:

> I've heard all of your platitudes. . . . "She's in a better place." And "This is all a part of a master plan." . . . Here's my favorite. "God looked down and saw the most beautiful rose, so beautiful that he picked it to have it in heaven, all for himself." Then there's the science, biocentrism, that we're all living and

dying in infinite universes all at the same time. And then there's the religion, the Christians and their salvation and the Buddhists and their Samsara and the Hindus with their forty-first sacrament.

He goes on to mention several more unhelpful platitudes, at least to his way of thinking. He sums it up by addressing death directly saying: "[Death] is a natural part of life. We shouldn't hate you. We shouldn't fear you. I guess we should just accept you, right? . . . It's all intellectual [expletive] because she's not here holding my [expletive] hand."

The healing view. It's hard to find fault with people who want to make the world better by alleviating suffering. Who could complain about people feeding starving children, providing medical care, or fighting against sex trafficking? And yet, some people *do* find fault.

Christopher Hitchens labeled Mother Teresa "a fanatic, a fundamentalist, and a fraud."[13] Australian feminist Germaine Greer deemed her a "'religious imperialist' who preyed on the most vulnerable in the name of harvesting souls for Jesus."[14] One can imagine someone from a Hindu perspective wanting Mother Teresa to stop rescuing people from dying in the streets because it could mess up the process of Karma. In other words, it is naive to think that everyone will agree on what is "good" or "harmful."

13 Christopher Hitchens, "Mommie Dearest," *Slate*, October 20, 2003, https://slate.com/.
14 Angus MacKinnon, "Catholic Icon Teresa Was Both Adored and Attacked," *Yahoo!News*, September 4, 2016, https://news.yahoo.com/.

Even so, the healing view has a lot going for it. It takes the problem of suffering seriously, recognizes the difficulties in fighting against it, and works diligently to improve people's circumstances. One could say the healing view is weak on the why question. It offers very little answer. And this causes a bigger problem. Without an overarching, larger perspective, the healing view provides less than adequate resources to compel persever-ance in the fight against suffering, sickness, and death. Without a metanarrative that provides a larger theoretical framework, it becomes easier and easier for people to lose enthusiasm in the fight. Without the conviction that a larger answer exists to the why question, pursuing answers to the how questions can lead to burnout.

The secular view. Whether this view is held rigorously by thorough-thinking philosophers or in less intellectual ways by people who just try to avoid the subject, the secular view is made attractive because of the pain and suffering around us. This view may seem to offer a better answer to the why question than reli-gious beliefs. Many people I talk to about their rejection of faith point to suffering as the cause. Anger provides an appearance of strength for some who abandon God. Some are honest enough to admit they're angry at a god they say they no longer believe in. Or they say, as one comedian put it, "I believe in God but I'm not a fan." The "stuff happens" answer to the why question satisfies them enough.

But, as I discussed with Aleena before the event with the Atheists' Society, it's in the realm of *how* questions where the secular view fails catastrophically. It offers few resources to help people handle disease, disaster, or death. Many have observed that Western culture, which is more secular than previous eras, is the most surprised by and therefore the least prepared for suffering.[15] Our current world has enough distractions to keep anyone far from serious contemplation—about anything, especially difficult topics like pain. That leaves people ill-equipped to offer support to others going through trials or to find inner strength for themselves to resist despair when facing the harsh realities of suffering.

The redemptive view. This is the view I hold, and I want you to consider (or reconsider) it carefully. In my opinion, it offers a better, more comprehensive answer to the why question than any other perspective. A good God created our good world with good gifts for us to enjoy. But we damaged the good world with our bad choices. While it may seem difficult to comprehend, human rebellion against God damages not only us but all creation. Thus, the reality we observe around us shows us the original creation's goodness (delightful sunsets, beautiful flowers, and magnificent landscapes) and gives us painful reminders of a fallen, broken world (natural disasters, disease, death, and crime).

But the redemptive view isn't without its difficulties. I find variances in suffering to be deeply troubling. Some people suffer their entire lives. Others never seem to experience a drop of pain. Some die young after battles against constant pain while others die peacefully in their sleep in their nineties. A tornado rips through a town, leveling houses and killing hundreds while, not far away,

15 See Keller, *Walking with God*, 26–27.

it leaves some houses and lives untouched. These inconsistencies disturb me greatly, and though I have a theology that tells me all creation suffers the consequences of sin, I still struggle with the ever-real, inadequately labeled problem of pain.

Despite these challenges in addressing the why question, it's the redemptive view that offers the best resources for the how questions, because it's founded on a historical event, not just a philosophical concept. Christians' entire system of belief rests on Jesus's resurrection. This establishes our hope in the afterlife on fact, not mere theory. If the resurrection is a fairy tale or lie, all of Christianity crumbles. But if it really happened, the Christian message points us to a world that will be recreated and a reality where pain and suffering will pass away. It provides joy and hope amid great suffering today and a certain future tomorrow.[16]

Hope in the Face of Death

I got to see the stark differences between clinging to belief and abandoning it through my friendship with Greg Boros. Despite the thirty-year gap in our ages, we knew we'd be close friends the first time we met. We both loved coffee, words, C. S. Lewis, the world of ideas, and the therapeutic power of laughter. We also shared the realities of heart disease.

My cardiac adventures included a heart attack and several surgeries that made sense, given my age and family history. Greg's heart problems made no sense at all, and not just because he was so young. My cardiac issues fit textbook descriptions. His defied

---

16 Lee Strobel's book *The Case for Christ* (Grand Rapids, MI: Zondervan, 1998) and the movie based on the book explore the evidence for the resurrection of Jesus far more than can be explored here.

all medical knowledge. Two years before we met, when Greg was twenty-one, he collapsed on a sidewalk without any warning. You might say he died that day when his heart stopped, but a fellow student who passed by knew CPR and brought him back to life. You could say he died again in the ambulance on the way to the hospital, but he was again revived. After testing and a lot of head-scratching, cardiologists determined Greg had a rare disease that defied categorization. They even considered naming it Greg Boros syndrome. After more than a week in the hospital, he got better, got married, and thought his medical trials were in the past. That's when he and I met and compared our lists of medications.

But Greg's heart problems hadn't disappeared. In the next few years, doctors determined that nothing short of a heart transplant could save his life. And at age twenty-five, he received that gift, which bought him ten more years. During that decade, Greg and his wife welcomed a son into their lives. They also developed a remarkable ministry on several college campuses. Greg loved to discuss issues of faith with skeptics. After all, it wasn't all that long ago that he also doubted and dismissed religious beliefs.

Before his heart problems, Greg wrestled with deep intellectual questions about God. He compared religions, investigated Jesus's life and words, and confronted his own predilection toward nihilistic hopelessness. Greg read arguments for and against the Bible's reliability. He studied the historical evidence for Jesus's resurrection. His thinking eventually brought him to embrace Christianity. He frequently told skeptics: "I came to believe in Christianity because it's true. I realized if the resurrection is real, everything is different from what I'd thought. God is real."

Greg's heart transplant solved some of his health issues. But for all the great advances in medical science, our bodies still struggle to tolerate implanted organs. The number of times Greg had to be admitted to the hospital for observation, tests, procedures, and adjustments to medication was staggering. Over time, anesthesia became less and less effective, and his pain became more and more excruciating.

If this weren't suffering enough, during the same decade, Greg also processed the horrors of being sexually abused as a child. If anyone had just cause to tell God to get lost, it was Greg Boros. He came close to doing just that. Along his journey came thoughts of suicide, a short stay in a mental hospital, years of therapy, and more tears than most shed in a lifetime. Some of us who had a front seat to his darkness feared for his sanity and life. I wish I could say that all Greg needed to hear was "God loves you" and it all turned around for him. But his journey required more mental, emotional, and spiritual wrestling matches than that. Remarkably, he didn't give up on the process he called "taking every thought down to the basement." He argued with God through colorfully worded prayers and wrestled with the disconnect between his theology (God is in control of everything.) and experience (It seems like God hates me.) Greg once told a roomful of university students:

> I've found out the tough way that there simply isn't anywhere you can go where Jesus isn't already there waiting for you. Down in the deepest, darkest basement, he was there waiting for me. I couldn't get depressed enough, I couldn't sin deeply enough, I couldn't hate and despair and pray for death intensely enough to drive him away.

Does the truth Greg discovered resolve all the mental puzzles we encounter with pain and suffering? Not for me. But it resolves them *enough* to bring hope and meaning in the darkness. Days before Greg died, he told his brother: "Life is very difficult, but Jesus is the only one who can be both Savior and friend. I'm not a Christian because that would make my life easy. I'm a Christian because it's true." Greg's widow has told me several times that he found immense comfort in the Bible's teaching that Jesus was "a man of sorrows and acquainted with grief." (Isa. 53:3). Greg and I spoke the day he died, and I could tell he'd been set free from the fear of death. He was sad to leave this earthly life but looked forward to the eternal one. Christians like Greg find profound comfort in these words from the New Testament:

> "Death is swallowed up in victory."
> "O death, where is your victory?
> O death, where is your sting?"

> The sting of death is sin, and the power of sin is the law. But thanks be to God, who gives us the victory through our Lord Jesus Christ.[17]

At Greg's funeral, some of his favorite words from C. S. Lewis were read:

> At present we are on the outside of the world, the wrong side of the door. We discern the freshness and purity of morning, but

---

17   1 Corinthians 15:54–57.

they do not make us fresh and pure. We cannot mingle with the splendours we see. But all the leaves of the New Testament are rustling with the rumour that it will not always be so. Some day, God willing, we shall get in.[18]

One of Greg's brothers read Revelation 21:3–4:

And I heard a loud voice from the throne saying, "Behold, the dwelling place of God is with man. He will dwell with them, and they will be his people, and God himself will be with them as their God. He will wipe away every tear from their eyes, and death shall be no more, neither shall there be mourning, nor crying, nor pain anymore, for the former things have passed away."

Questioning the Problem of Pain

Pain is a problem for everyone. We must find some way to deal with it—in both our thinking and our living. We've seen that there are only a few ways to handle this issue, and all of them feel incomplete. So the question is this: Which incomplete answer will you embrace to help you with the problem of evil?

Is suffering always someone's fault? An illusion we need to reframe? A problem we can eradicate? Do we live in a chaotic, purposeless, meaningless world without any design that, oddly, has outbreaks of beauty, splendor, and wonder? Or do we live in a good world created by a purposeful and personal God, with evidence of harm done to that world? One writer summed up

18 C. S. Lewis, *The Weight of Glory: And Other Addresses*, rev. ed. (1980; repr., San Francisco: HarperCollins, 2001), 44.

the choice like this: "The alternative to disappointment with God seems to be disappointment without God."[19]

I would've liked to share some of these thoughts with Aleena when she told me about her uncle. Perhaps I would've added that the presence of beauty in this life must be considered alongside the problem of pain. The fact that she loved her uncle so much, and that he made her smile, may point to a tapestry woven with purpose, joy, and beauty. In the next chapter, we'll turn to that important theme.

19 Philip Yancey, *Disappointment with God: Three Questions No One Asks Aloud* (New York: HarperCollins, 1988), 311.

6

The Question of Pleasure

*What If There's More to Beauty
Than Meets the Eye?*

JERRAM BARRS FELT he had no other choice.

> I was overwhelmed with emptiness, longing for escape, and the
> only escape appeared to be death. I ordered my little affairs,
> caught a bus out of Manchester, and walked to Alderley Edge,
> a high cliff in the Cheshire hills, with the fixed intention of
> stepping over and ending my life.[1]

What brought Jerram to such a moment of despair? Jerram grew
up surrounded by books.

> My parents read aloud to us every night, right up until we
> went off to college. From them I gained a delight in good

---

1 Jerram Barrs, *The Heart of Evangelism* (Wheaton, IL: Crossway, 2001), 120.

writing wherever it was found, whether in children's books, fiction, fantasy, or poetry. Great literature deals with the human condition in all its sorrow and joy. It asks difficult questions that confront all people and sometimes it even answers those questions accurately.[2]

In college, Jerram took as many literature courses as he could, hoping to hear learned professors expound on the meaning of life from great books. But his hopes were dashed as, one after another, his professors ignored the profound questions literature raises, almost admitting there are no answers. Instead, they delved into technicalities like the "form and structure and skills that make great writing work. . . . [They had] no passion for the content of the texts we studied."[3] It was as if his teachers wanted him to admit the pointlessness of human existence.

Jerram immersed himself in the dominant artistic theme of 1960s Britain: angst. He read books by Hardy, Sartre, Camus, and Hemingway; plays by Ibsen, Beckett, and Ionesco. He watched films by Bergman, Antonioni, and Fellini, and he listened to the music of Strauss, Dylan, and the Rolling Stones. Again and again, he landed in a mood of hopelessness and despair.

Despair finally brought Jerram to the cliff, ready to end his misery.

There, one step from eternity, I was held back by the beauty of the natural world around me. It was January, and it was cold with a harsh wind; but it was sunny, and the skies were clear

2 Barrs, *The Heart of Evangelism*, 119.
3 Barrs, *The Heart of Evangelism*, 120.

and blue. The trees were bare, but they still had beauty; there were no flowers, but the grass was green and alive. . . . If there could be such beauty even in winter, surely there had to be some answer to my questions besides meaninglessness.[4]

Jerram went back to his campus and started conversing with fellow students about his questions. Eventually, he met a Christian who invited him to a Bible study on the Old Testament book of Ecclesiastes. The book begins with these despairing words:

"Meaningless! Meaningless!"
   says the Teacher.
"Utterly meaningless!
   Everything is meaningless."[5]

You might think that would put Jerram back at the cliff. But Ecclesiastes grabbed his attention in two powerful ways. First, the literary, poetic beauty of the book impressed him. It had something weighty to say, and it said it with style. Second, the book's ideas convinced him to read other parts of the Bible.

This sober realism in Ecclesiastes was God's means of convincing me to take His Word seriously and to begin to consider His Word as words of truth, truth that makes sense of the world in which we live, truth that fits like a glove on the hand of reality.[6]

---

4 Barrs, *The Heart of Evangelism*, 121.
5 Ecclesiastes 1:2 NIV.
6 Barrs, *The Heart of Evangelism*, 123.

Jerram is not the only person who's been arrested by beauty, pleasure, or wonder and then asked where this grandeur comes from. Others have pointed to music, art, story, and other means of transcendence as the triggers that move them from doubt to delight.

Paintings on Walls

Christopher Hitchens's brother, Peter, says it was two paintings that challenged his atheist convictions. He found the contrast between beauty and ugliness suggestive of larger issues of good and evil.

Peter and Christopher were raised by the same parents only a few years apart. They attended the same boarding school and saw the same hypocrisy. Like Christopher, Peter also embraced atheism. He begins his memoir, *The Rage against God: How Atheism Led Me to Faith*, this way: "I set fire to my Bible on the playing fields of my Cambridge boarding school one bright, windy spring afternoon in 1967. I was fifteen years old."[7] Years later, he saw things differently, admitting that though he "had some good reasons for refusing some of it [Christianity], [his] mistake was to dispense with it all, indiscriminately."[8]

Peter's story turns on the ugliness of atheism. Sometimes it was atheists' unkindness toward people of faith. For all their talk about religion poisoning everything, Peter saw far too many atheists poisoned by their own faith-like commitment to unbelief. He highlights Virginia Woolf's harsh words about T. S. Eliot's conversion as one of many examples. She wrote to her sister, "I have had

---

7 Peter Hitchens, *The Rage against God: How Atheism Led Me to Faith* (Grand Rapids, MI: Zondervan, 2010), 17.

8 Hitchens, *The Rage against God*, 10.

a most shameful and distressing interview with poor dear Tom Eliot, who may be called dead to us all from this day forward. . . . A corpse would seem to me more credible than he is."[9]

The bulk of Peter's disillusionment with atheism came when he lived in Moscow. He saw a government system built on a godless worldview. In contrast to the positive descriptions he'd read in books, he encountered physical ugliness, economic inequities, rampant corruption, ubiquitous dishonesty, and the dehumanizing treatment of the nation's citizens. Peter began to wonder if Soviet Russia accurately embodied atheism or had devolved into an aberration of it. He wanted to find favor with the atheist state, but when he saw how cruelty permeated Soviet life, he reluctantly and unhappily concluded, "Enormous and intrusive totalitarian state power, especially combined with militant egalitarianism, is an enemy of civility, of consideration, and even of unenlightened self-interest."[10]

Later in his memoir, he says, "I have seldom seen a more powerful argument for the fallen nature of man, and his inability to achieve perfection, than those countries in which man set himself up to replace God with the state."[11] What nudged Peter Hitchens across the line from doubt to faith wasn't a dramatic and emotional experience, intense intellectual study, or close relationships with people of faith, though those play legitimate roles in others' journeys. For Peter, a lover of art, architecture, and music, it was seeing two paintings—*The Last Judgment* by Rogier van der Weyden and *The Prodigal Son* by Thomas Hart Benton. You

9   Hitchens, *The Rage against God*, 24.
10 Hitchens, *The Rage against God*, 91.
11 Hitchens, *The Rage against God*, 152.

can Google these strikingly different paintings. They drew Peter Hitchens to consider alienation from God and the loss of family connections. Ultimately, they pushed Peter in an unpredictable and, to some extent, unwanted direction.

Art can do that. So can natural beauty. It can awaken, clarify, or convict. Pleasures of many kinds can raise questions about existence. They point us beyond ourselves.

The Beauty of the Stars

When I first visited Mike Summers at his office, I smiled at the bumper sticker on his door: "My other vehicle is on its way to Pluto." As a professor of physics and astronomy at George Mason University and a consultant for NASA, Mike was part of a team counting down the days and years until their exploratory probe would reach the small planet three billion miles from earth. The journey would take almost a decade.

I've met with Mike many times, and I always feel his enthusiasm for scientific discovery. He battles autoimmune diseases that sap his energy, but he never fails to rise above and gush with enthusiasm about recent findings in space.

Mike loves to tell of new planets we've found, of vast amounts of water on some of these planets, of the new tools we're inventing for explorations in the far reaches of space, and of how many more planetary scientists our world has now than when he began his career. He goes on with an ever-increasing smile on his face. Mike uses religious words like *awe* when he talks about journal articles on stars and planets. He's always loved exploring. It was asking questions about the heavens that made him rethink the teachings he received at his childhood church.

Mike Summers was raised in a rural community where education wasn't valued. His family's fundamentalist church taught that "you had to choose between God and science. You couldn't believe in both." They said evolution was pronounced "evil-ution."

As a curious child, Mike had lots of questions, but his Sunday school teachers told him to stop asking them and "just have faith." That only raised more questions! What is faith? What is science? And why can't we believe that the God who gave us brains to think also made a world worth thinking about?

One day, when Mike was still quite young, his pastor made a special visit to his home to ask his parents to tell their son to stop asking questions in church. So, by the time Mike reached fourteen, he knew the fundamentalist, anti-intellectual brand of Christianity couldn't possibly be true. He had little to do with the faith for the next fifteen years. During his undergraduate and masters-level studies, formal religion was nonexistent for him. Though he'd never doubted there must be a god, he wondered why he (or any intelligent person) should listen to someone who claimed to know things about Jesus's life long ago but spoke gibberish about the physical world we live in now.

Years later, while pursuing his PhD at Caltech, Mike discovered a different kind of faith. One of his first professors was a Christian who found no conflict with doing rigorous scientific research during the week and worshiping God on Sunday. That opened the door for Mike to reconsider God, faith, and science.

Mike is now a committed Christian. He loves to marvel at what we can learn about God by studying the universe of planets, stars, and galaxies. "Our God has crafted the laws that govern these objects in a way that allows us to have a rich life on Earth."[12] Mike will tell you, in many ways, that the physical universe is carefully crafted, not randomly thrown together.

As I've listened to Mike share his story, three themes have emerged.

First, Mike now draws distinctions between the Christianity of the Bible and the faith of his upbringing. The text of Genesis doesn't demand the narrow interpretations his church insisted upon. Nothing in the Bible's first few chapters gives us definitive statements about the age of the earth or universe. The creation account seems far more interested in *who* did the creating than it is in how long it took him.

Second, Mike discovered an intellectually rigorous Christianity that contrasted with the shallow variety from his upbringing. Through reading the New Testament accounts and thoughtful writers like Lewis, he felt challenged by the faith's complexity. There was a world of difference between the faith he read about and the religion in which he was raised.

Third, Mike grew in appreciation for science while recognizing its limitations. "Science is a tool for discovering the nature of the universe—nothing more, nothing less." And while we continue to grow in knowledge about the universe every single day, we must admit we are surprised countless times along the way.

Mike now lectures about the compatibility between science and faith. His Christian convictions grow the more he learns about stars and planets. He marvels at the vast universe God has crafted. He likes to quote Psalm 19:1, "The heavens declare the glory of

---

12 Mike's story and quotes from his talks are adapted from his unpublished manuscript "How Big Is Our God?"

God," then share the many new discoveries we've made about the heavens. He never grows tired of challenging both skeptics and believers: "I encourage you to choose to see the universe the way it is. You might see a bigger God."

A Larger Story

You may have heard that C. S. Lewis was a professor of English literature at Oxford and Cambridge. Many people know him as the creator of The Chronicles of Narnia, but few know his journey from atheism to Christianity.[13] Lewis's mother died when he was nine years old. That tragedy prompted a rejection of his parents' Christian faith. Lewis had prayed for God to heal his mother, but she died anyway. So Lewis gave up on God and persisted in unbelief for more than twenty years. Academic training only sharpened his mind for rigorous arguments against theism. Later he wrote, "I maintained that God did not exist and I was angry at God for not existing."[14]

But amid this unbelief, Lewis was drawn to story. He loved Norse mythology. Through his days at Oxford and into his time as a professor, he loved how mythology delved into struggles between right and wrong, the need for rescue, and the role of sacrifice. Lewis befriended J. R. R. Tolkien and other writers

---

13 For Lewis's book-length account of his faith journey, see *Surprised by Joy: The Shape of My Early Life* (New York: HarperCollins, 1955; repr., San Francisco: HarperCollins, 2017); or one of several biographies, such as George Sayer, *Jack: A Life of C. S. Lewis* (Wheaton, IL: Crossway, 2005), or Harry Lee Poe, *The Making of C. S. Lewis: From Atheist to Apologist (1918–1945)* (Wheaton, IL: Crossway, 2021), the second part of a trilogy on Lewis's life.

14 C. S. Lewis, *Surprised by Joy: The Shape of My Early Life* (New York: HarperCollins, 1955), 115.

who challenged him to rethink the Christian story. They pointed to an inconsistency between Lewis's love for mythology and his rejection of any larger narrative. During a long conversation, Tolkien and another friend, Hugo Dyson, suggested that perhaps we love myths because there is a grand, overarching "myth" from which the lesser myths derive. Years later, Lewis summed up his inner contradiction: "Nearly all that I loved I believed to be imaginary. Nearly all that I believed to be real I thought grim and meaningless."[15] After that conversation, Lewis wrote:

> Now what Dyson and Tolkien showed me was this: that if I met the idea of sacrifice in a Pagan story I didn't mind it at all: again, that if I met the idea of a god sacrificing himself to himself . . . , I liked it very much and was mysteriously moved by it. . . . The reason was that in Pagan stories I was prepared to feel the myth as profound and suggestive of meanings beyond my grasp even though I could not say in cold prose "what it meant."
>
> Now the story of Christ is simply a true myth: a myth working on us in the same way as the others, but with this tremendous difference that *it really happened*.[16]

Some people's indirect journeys of belief through terrains of doubt seem uneventful, plateaued, or stagnant until an event or an idea serves as a tipping point. Often that event is a tragedy or trauma. For Lewis, it was the opposite. It was the undeniable reality of beauty that flipped his worldview. The conversation

15 Lewis, *Surprised by Joy*, 11.
16 Paul Ford, ed., *Yours, Jack: Spiritual Direction from C. S. Lewis* (New York: HarperCollins, 2008), 28, emphasis original.

about myth was the tipping point. Once he conceded that a larger myth could be the source of all lesser myths, he was more open to Christianity. He investigated it with all the intellectual skill he had honed for decades. What resulted was a two-stage conversion from atheism to theism and then to Christianity. The first stage felt far from pleasant.

> You must picture me alone in that room at Magdalen, night after night, feeling, whenever my mind lifted even for a second from my work, the steady, unrelenting approach of Him whom I so earnestly desired not to meet. That which I greatly feared had at last come upon me. In the Trinity Term of 1929 I gave in, and admitted that God was God, and knelt and prayed: perhaps, that night, the most dejected and reluctant convert in all England.[17]

It took a while to progress to Christian conviction, the culmination of which he recounted as a remarkably unemotional and rather mundane event: "I was driven to Whipsnade one sunny morning. When we set out I did not believe that Jesus Christ is the Son of God, and when we reached the zoo I did."[18]

The Transcendence of Music

My indirect journey of belief met its tipping point after a major tragedy. As I described in chapter 4, I first tried to connect with God through Judaism. Then, I went off to college and thought little about God. Instead, I majored in beer, with a minor in cynicism. My official university registration claimed music as my major, but

17 Lewis, *Surprised by Joy*, 279.
18 Lewis, *Surprised by Joy*, 290.

given the hours spent at drunken parties, watching Woody Allen movies, or reading existentialist literature, it's safer to conclude alcohol and absurdity took priority. I'd given up hope that Judaism could provide the answers I was looking for. I'd mostly given up looking for answers anywhere, assuming life was meaningless.

But music kept drawing me back toward the transcendent. I held on to slivers of hope by attending performances by the Philadelphia Orchestra every Saturday night. I longed to find some piece of music I could claim as a link to the eternal. Dvořák, Rachmaninoff, or Tchaikovsky came close, but every piece also brought disappointment. The magic dissipated even before the music drew to its finale. My subway rides back to my dorm room brought despondency and despair.

Then, one Sunday night, two friends were playing a game of toy basketball in the sixth-floor lounge of our high-rise dorm. They bounced off each other going for a rebound, and one crashed through a plate glass window and plunged to his death six stories below. Forty years later, I still gasp at the horror of that night. As I sat at his funeral a few days later, I knew I needed to get answers about life's meaning, because comedy, cynicism, and cocktails weren't helping me.

Inexplicably, I'd brought that copy of the New Testament given to me years before along with me to college. I found it buried in my closet, dusted it off, and started reading. I also dug into the other book those friends told me about—C. S. Lewis's *Mere Christianity*.[19]

---

19 If you've never read Lewis's classic, you owe it to yourself to read at least the book's first two sections, "Right and Wrong as a Clue to the Meaning of the Universe" and "What Christians Believe." This book has helped many sort out issues of faith, and it continues to be a bestseller around the world. Some of its content may seem dated

Matthew, the writer of the first book in the New Testament, was Jewish, and he wrote his account of Jesus's life with a Jewish audience in mind. He quoted from the Hebrew Scriptures, building an argument to show that Jesus was the promised Messiah. Matthew's book struck me as the exact opposite of the antisemitic writing my rabbi had warned about. It seemed overwhelmingly Jewish.

Lewis put exclamation points on what I was concluding as I read Matthew, but it was Lewis's insights about beauty that intrigued me most. It was as if he'd been sitting next to me in the balcony of Philadelphia's Academy of Music taking in those concerts. Lewis spoke of disappointments in life and how we might handle them:

> The books or the music in which we thought the beauty was located will betray us if we trust to [sic] them; it was not *in* them, it only came *through* them, and what came through them was longing. These things—the beauty, the memory of our own past—are good images of what we really desire; but if they are mistaken for the thing itself, they turn into dumb idols, breaking the hearts of their worshippers. For they are not the thing itself; they are only the scent of a flower we have not found, the echo of a tune we have not heard, news from a country we have never yet visited.[20]

I loved how Lewis expanded his discussion beyond beauty to all of life. Whether it's an experience, a job, a spouse, or anything

---

to twenty-first-century readers, but don't let that dissuade you from giving it a fair hearing.

20 C. S. Lewis, *The Weight of Glory: and Other Addresses*, rev. ed. (1980; repr., New York: HarperCollins, 2001), 30–31, emphasis original.

else, we often sense a letdown—even with the very best in life. Lewis said we can handle these disappointments in one of three ways. We can keep chasing other experiences, jobs, or spouses, only to find more disappointments. We can become cynics and give up any hope of finding satisfaction beyond the mundane. Or there's "the Christian way," which concludes, "If I find in myself a desire which no experience in this world can satisfy, the most probable explanation is that I was made for another world."[21] That insight put a frame around all of life for me, and it pointed me to the God of that "other world." Lewis's words transformed a multitude of disappointments—in music, relationships, experiences, accomplishments, you name it—into pointers to the God who made our world filled with pleasures, beauty, delights, and delicious food. Yes, even food can be a pointer to the God who gave us the senses of smell and taste.

Lewis persuaded me I was longing to find God. Matthew showed me I needed to find him. Together they convinced me that Jesus is the Savior who brings us to God.

This brings us to one more important milestone:

We need perspectives within us that can account for the beauty around us.

Questioning Beauty

Do you relate to these experiences of longing? If so, where does your longing show up—when seeing a beautiful sunset, standing before a Van Gogh painting, hearing a captivating song, or staring

---

21 C. S. Lewis, *Mere Christianity* (New York: HarperCollins, 1955), 136–37.

up at the sky? Is it in reading a well-told tale, savoring a delicious meal, or laughing at a friend's joke? Which seems more likely—that displays of natural beauty point to a supernatural source or that they are coincidences in a random world? How have you reconciled the experiences of pleasure in your life with the beliefs you hold about meaning, faith, and God?

In the previous chapter we explored the problem of pain. In this chapter we observed the wonder of beauty. How do you make sense of these realities occurring in the same world? If you've ever had the privilege of visiting the Louvre in Paris, you probably braved the crowds to get a glimpse of the statue of Venus de Milo. Millions have been captivated by the woman's physical beauty displayed in stunningly smooth marble. They've also been disturbed by seeing her arms broken off. Somehow the damage done to her arms doesn't destroy the aesthetic pleasure of viewing the sculpture as a whole. But it does cause a conflicted experience—such beauty, marred by such violence.

I doubt if anyone has ever stood in front of that masterpiece and asked, "Why did the sculptor break off the arms?" More likely, everyone concludes the beautiful parts are the work of a master artist and the broken parts are the results of someone or something else—either a destructive criminal or a natural catastrophe.

We need a unified perspective on created beauty and marred ugliness that can make sense of both. The Christian faith provides that. It points to a good God who made a beautiful world with pleasures for people to enjoy. But it also recognizes damage caused by sinful people. Ultimately, it points to a process of restoration that has already begun and will continue forever.

But a few questions still remain.

Conclusion

How Will You Respond?

I'VE POSED A LOT OF QUESTIONS, and I will ask a few more as I bring this book to a conclusion. But first, I want to tell one more story.

A religious Jewish man named Nicodemus came to meet Jesus at night. Why at night? So he wouldn't be seen by his fellow religious leaders. Sometimes peer pressure thwarts the pursuit of spiritual truth. It was no surprise that Nicodemus had heard about Jesus. Jesus drew crowds wherever he went. Not long before this nighttime chat, Jesus had turned water into wine at a wedding. It's hard to ignore a miracle. Perhaps that's what propelled Nicodemus to risk social alienation and pursue Jesus.

When you read the account of this interaction (and I do suggest you read the entire section in the third chapter of John's Gospel), you'll see that Nicodemus started and finished this exchange unsure of what was going on. He didn't know how to formulate a question to ask. So he began with something like flattery: "Rabbi, we know that you are a teacher come from God, for no one can do these signs that you do unless God is with him."[1] We need to resist the temptation to criticize Nicodemus for his vagueness. Sometimes spiritual journeys pass through confusion before they arrive at clarity.

Jesus offered what might seem like a non sequitur: "Truly, truly, I say to you, unless one is born again he cannot see the kingdom of God."[2] Not only does this statement seem out of place: it could have insulted someone as righteous as Nicodemus. We have no reason to doubt his spiritual credentials. We're told he was a "teacher of Israel."[3] You don't earn that kind of title without an impressive resume. But Jesus's point must not be missed. If even Nicodemus needed a new birth, one that could not be achieved through heredity or human effort, then every person who has lived needs a spiritual birth.[4]

To clarify his point, Jesus added that when someone experiences new birth, it's like the wind. You can't quite understand all that's going on when the wind blows, but there's no doubt it's blowing. Spiritual journeys have their rational components—like when Alex (in chap. 1) read the book of Romans, or when Barry (in chap. 3) read critiques of atheism. But they also have their emotional, or nonmeasurable, aspects, like when Peter Hitchens viewed works of art, or when Jerram Barrs didn't jump off the cliff.

If you have a good friendship with a Christian, it might be worth asking him or her what it was like to become a Christian.

1 John 3:2.
2 John 3:3.
3 John 3:10.
4 See John 1:9–18, especially verses 12–13 for an elaboration on this theme.

That's a different question from *What convinced you to believe?* Both questions have great value. Images of spiritual transformation can clarify and intensify the cognitive truths behind them. Throughout the centuries, Christians have suggested a variety of images to describe their internal experiences of conversion. For some it's like walking into a lit room after groping about in darkness. For others it's like getting rescued from drowning or waking up after a long sleep, or like a concrete statue transforming into a living person or rebels laying down their arms or finding buried treasure or breathing clean air after almost suffocating.

The interchange between Jesus and Nicodemus reached a climax with some of Jesus's most frequently quoted (but not always understood) words: "For God loved the world in this way: He gave his one and only Son, so that everyone who believes in him will not perish but have eternal life."[5] He continued with words that get far less airtime:

> For God did not send his Son into the world to condemn the world, but in order that the world might be saved through him. Whoever believes in him is not condemned, but whoever does not believe is condemned already, because he has not believed in the name of the only Son of God.[6]

As if that were not pointed enough, Jesus added this stinger: "This is the judgment: the light has come into the world, and people loved the darkness rather than the light because their works

5 John 3:16 CSB.
6 John 3:17–18.

were evil."[7] We must not miss this crucial point: in addition to cognitive and emotional components, the new birth must also include a humbling one—repentance. It comes when people acknowledge they've thought or said or done things worthy of condemnation by a holy God. They realize and admit that they, at times, have loved darkness more than light and that some of their deeds are evil.

The curtain comes down on this nighttime scene, and we don't know what Nicodemus thought. Our best guess is that he still felt puzzled. But that's not the last we hear from that teacher of Israel. He shows up again several chapters later in John's account of Jesus's life. This time he seems to have progressed in his willingness to risk rejection from his peers.

Debates about Jesus's identity were raging. (Some things never change.) Jesus's question "Who do you say that I am?"[8] continues to challenge anyone willing to dig into this pivotal question. In John 7, some people identified merely as "servants" want the chief priests to answer that very question. "No one ever spoke like this man!" they claim.[9] The leaders dodge the question by attacking those who have asked it. "Have you also been deceived?"[10] But Nicodemus tries to inject a voice of reason into the clamor. "We should hear more from this Jesus" is the gist of his appeal. But he receives the same flack as the servants. Once again, the scene comes to an end without resolution. But Nicodemus has clearly progressed from clueless to curious.

---

7   John 3:19.
8   Mark 8:29.
9   John 7:46.
10 John 7:47.

He comes on stage one final time—after Jesus has died—as recorded in John 19. A disciple of Jesus, Joseph of Arimathea, asks if he can take Jesus's body off the cross and provide a proper burial. John tells us that Nicodemus helps him with that painful task. No longer hiding by dark of night, he takes a public stand for anyone to see. Has Nicodemus become a disciple like Joseph? Has he progressed from clueless to curious to convinced? That seems to be the case, although John allows us to wonder. And why not? Perhaps Nicodemus's indirect journey perfectly embodies the image of wind that Jesus used to describe the process of becoming a Christian. Perhaps Nicodemus's story prompts us to examine our own views about Jesus and propels us to progress in our spiritual journey.

The Most Helpful Questions

What could it have been like for Nicodemus to dare to meet with Jesus that first time? He had to question some deeply established convictions and allow himself to wonder if some of his basic assumptions might have been wrong. He might have asked himself some "what if" questions:

- What if the things I've believed for so long have been flawed?
- What if the things I've denied are true?
- What if I'm not as right or righteous as I've assumed?
- What if I need something that I can't provide or manufacture for myself?

"What if" questions may be the most helpful ones we can ask regarding faith. I heard variations of that question in the many conversations I've had with people who progressed from terrains of doubt to paths of belief. I look back and see these were some of the most helpful questions I allowed myself to ask:

- What if life really isn't one big joke?
- What if music is a pointer instead of an end?
- What if what I've been taught about Jesus isn't accurate?
- What if the New Testament fits well with the Old Testament—like a hand and glove?

Georgiana dared ask, "What if there really is a source of unconditional love?" Contrary to all her experiences of abuse and performance-based acceptance, she found a way out of hopelessness and despair. Our world cries out for this kind of love through the songs we sing, the movies we watch, and the relationships we try to make work. Something inside us wants to believe lofty exaltations of love like Victor Hugo's: "The supreme happiness of life is the conviction that we are loved; loved for ourselves—say rather, loved in spite of ourselves."[11]

What if there really is that kind of love because it came from a perfect lover, about whom it was written, "God is love"?[12]

Susan dared to ask, "What if there really is forgiveness for all the wrongs I've done?" After trying to find serenity and peace without forgiveness, she wondered if what she'd heard about the spiritual realm was misguided. What if she really needed the kind of forgiveness that could only come from a perfect sacrifice? What if we can't really get our good deeds to outweigh our bad

11 Victor Hugo, *Les Misérables* (New York: Signet, 2013), 166.
12 1 John 4:8.

deeds? What if we don't need to get our good deeds to outweigh our bad deeds because a perfect solution has been offered that is not based on our good deeds? What if there really is a source of joy that's so overflowing that it transcends circumstances, failures, and even our greatest successes?

Greg dared to cling to answers to questions like "What if there really is life after death?" "What if Jesus's resurrection ensures my resurrection?" "What if all the pain and disease and evil I've seen will be wiped away because Jesus took the punishment for all that?" After doubting his own doubts, Greg landed on the conviction that God's truth is more certain than his questions.

What if you told God you wanted that kind of love, joy, and hope? What if you confessed you couldn't produce those virtues on your own? What if you admitted you still have questions but were willing to trust in the answers you've received so far: that God really is who he says he is, that Jesus really did pay for your sins, and that you were willing to follow him despite the cost?

One Final Question

Questions, by their very nature, call for a response. It seems only right to save the last question in this book for one Jesus posed.[13] When he spoke about eternal life, he began with a bold claim only he could make: "I am the resurrection and the life. Whoever believes in me, though he die, yet shall he live, and everyone who lives and believes in me shall never die."

Then he asked the question everyone must answer: "Do you believe this?"

13 John 11:25–26. It's best to read all of John 11 to feel the force of this claim and the question.

Appendix

What Are Some Good Next Steps?

SPIRITUAL JOURNEYS PROGRESS best with travel companions. If this book has sparked a desire to continue your trek, seek out some people who have been on the trail for a while. Perhaps a Christian friend gave you this book. Discussing it with that friend is a good next step. Finding a community of believers in a local church would also serve you well.

In addition to the resources I've cited or recommended earlier in this book, here are some more as you continue your journey.

If you want to hear some thoughtful answers to important questions about the Christian faith, Timothy Keller's *The Reason for God: Belief in an Age of Skepticism* is a good place to start. Keller has shaped my thinking almost as much as C. S. Lewis has. Several of Rebecca McLaughlin's books, especially *Confronting Christianity: 12 Hard Questions for the World's Largest Religion*, take on contemporary concerns with clarity and empathy. If you're in your teenage years, her book *10 Questions Every Teen Should Ask (and Answer) about Christianity* is ideal.

If watching videos works better for you than reading books, you can find quite a few helpful ones at www.christianityexplored .org. If you're ready to become a Christian and want guidance for taking this life-transforming, eternity-changing step, the video "The Story" can guide you; see https://thestoryfilm.com.

If you're philosophically minded and don't mind diving into the deep end of the intellectual pool, Paul Gould's *A Good and True Story: Eleven Clues to Understanding Our Universe and Your Place in It* and Gregory Ganssle's *Our Deepest Desires: How the Christian Story Fulfills Human Aspirations* will be well worth your effort.

Only slightly less rigorous are Gavin Ortlund's *Why God Makes Sense in a World That Doesn't* and Glen Scrivener's very engaging book *The Air We Breathe: How We All Came to Believe in Freedom, Kindness, Progress, and Equality.*

If the problem of evil is particularly vexing for you, C. S. Lewis's *The Problem of Pain*, Peter Kreeft's *Making Sense Out of Suffering*, and Timothy Keller's *Walking with God through Pain and Suffering* can help.

Though I only touched on LGBT+ issues through Thomas's story, the issues are too complex and important to leave there. Here are some very helpful resources:

- Sam Allberry's *Is God Anti-Gay?* and his more recent *Why Does God Care Who I Sleep With?*
- Glynn Harrison's *A Better Story: God, Sex and Human Flourishing*
- Jackie Hill Perry's *Gay Girl: Good God: The Story of Who I Was, and Who God Has Always Been*

- Rachel Gilson's *Born Again This Way: Coming Out, Coming to Faith, and What Comes Next*

If you want to hear some challenging perspectives from someone who does not identify as a Christian, consider Louise Perry's *The Case against the Sexual Revolution: A New Guide to Sex in the 21st Century.*

If you've recently become a Christian and feel a little intimidated by trying to read the Bible, Gary Millar's *Read This First: A Simple Guide to Getting the Most from the Bible* and Tim Chester's *Life with Jesus: A Discipleship Course for Every Christian* could help greatly.

My two favorite online resources, jam-packed with more articles, videos, and blogs than you can exhaust, are www.thegospel coalition.org and www.cslewisinstitute.org. If I can answer questions or offer insights for your quest, please do not hesitate to email me at Questioningfaithnow@gmail.com.

General Index

absolute certainty, 44, 59, 60
acceptance, worship of, 23–24, 29, 40
affection, 29, 31
affirmation, 31, 40
alcohol, 11
Allah, 75, 81
Allberry, Sam, 126
all-religions-are-the-same argument, 65, 74
America, anti-institutional and spiritually self-focused, 37
Angels Landing Hike (Zion National Park), 1–2, 10
anger, 17
Anselm, 56
anti-theist, 8
art, 104, 105–6
astronomy, 106
atheism, 9, 71
   doubts of, 45–48
   and grief, 81–82
   and moral judgments, 12
   ugliness of, 104–5
atonement, 68
Augustine, 56

Bannister, Andy, 75
Barrs, Jerram, 101–4
beauty
   accounting for, 114–15
   arrested by, 104, 115
   of natural world, 14, 17, 102–3, 106
   in this life, 100
Benton, Thomas Hart, 105
blind-men-and-the-elephant story, 61–65
Boros, Greg, 95–99
Boswell, James, 17
Buddhists, 78, 84, 85, 92
Burton, Tara Isabella, 35–37

certainty, 44–45, 56–57, 59, 60
chattel slavery, 89n9
Christianity
   as opiate of the masses, 66
   on redemptive view of suffering, 87
clinging to Christ in suffering, 88–89
coherence, 57–60
Collateral Beauty (film), 86, 91–92
confidence, 59, 60
   amid doubts, 54–56

Scripture Index

TGC | THE GOSPEL COALITION

The Gospel Coalition (TGC) supports the church in making disciples of all nations, by providing gospel-centered resources that are trusted and timely, winsome and wise.

Guided by a Council of more than 40 pastors in the Reformed tradition, TGC seeks to advance gospel-centered ministry for the next generation by producing content (including articles, podcasts, videos, courses, and books) and convening leaders (including conferences, virtual events, training, and regional chapters).

In all of this we want to help Christians around the world better grasp the gospel of Jesus Christ and apply it to all of life in the 21st century. We want to offer biblical truth in an era of great confusion. We want to offer gospel-centered hope for the searching.

Join us by visiting TGC.org so you can be equipped to love God with all your heart, soul, mind, and strength, and to love your neighbor as yourself.

TGC.org

Also Available from TGC

For more information, visit **crossway.org**.